LE GUIDE

FOR THE INDEPENDENT
MOTORWAY TRAVELLER IN FRANCE

by

Karol Libura

LE GUIDE PUBLICATIONS
London

Published by Le Guide Publications, London.

First published May 1986 as
The Motorway to the Sun,

Second edition published June 1987 as
Autoroutes to the Sun,

This edition published March 1989,
Reprinted with minor amendments, April 1990.

© Copyright 1986 M.K.Libura, London

ISBN 0 9511254 2 7

Printed and bound in Great Britain
by
Drydens Printers, London.

om the Publisher:

ou are likely to experience courtesy of others
 being courteous.

njoy the guide,
hope it will serve you well.

ONNE CHANCE

ON VOYAGE

arol Libura

CONTENTS

he actual routes (going South);

he actual routes (going North);

LOOK NO FURTHER

Typical comments upon the publication:

From the Press;

" ... a wonderfully comprehensive and easily understoc guide " – Practical Motorist Magazine,

" It is a new style guide for motorists. I have never seen guide which explains itself so easily" – East Kent Mercury

" It contains all the information you need to make the most the motorways to the South " – Practical Caravan Magazin Britain's biggest selling caravan magazine,

" ...a handy little book which no one using the Fren Autoroute from Calais to the Riviera should be without " – Tl Times,

" The icing on the cake is the seemingly limitless invaluat information to the motorist. It's got to be a must for anyol motoring in France. And it's a change to find a guide book th doesn't fall apart with a bit of wear!" – Evening Ech Bournemouth,

" ... clearly with the benefit of much wheels-on experience. has to be an essential occupant of the glovebox of eve France bound car" – Motor Magazine,

" ... is worth every penny to the traveller South " – Carava Life Magazine. The Magazine For Caravanners,

" It is an invaluable guide for the traveller through France " Your Car Magazine,

" His tips for staying safe on European roads are obvious written from experience. It has to be an essential addition the caravanner's holiday list " – Popular Caravan Magazin

and there are more, to quote them would mean to repeat the above.

From the users of the guide;

" ...as regular visitors to the South of France for very mai years we have studied your guide carefully and we think it excellent and certainly recommend it " – Frank and Pame Reade from Liverpool,

" ...we found the information invaluable on our journey down through France, and we await your next edition with interest " - B.C.Russell from Sunbury-on-Thames,

" I must say that although we travel up and down the Autoroute yearly to either Menton or Perpignan, we did find the book most useful and very accurate " – Inga E.Muir from Stockton-on-Tees, Cleveland,

" I would like to say that I found this book very informative, interesting and colourful. The routes are clear and concise with special mention of the signs to follow en route to Paris and also through Paris which I found to be helpful especially for the first time traveller going South.

In conclusion I would not travel to France without this book in the future, and I look forward to seeing further editions in the years to come " – Linda Sands from Wemyss Bay in Scotland,

"We were delighted by its accuracy and usefulness" – Dorothy Skelly, Doncaster,

" Many thanks for the Guide, it is excellent and answers all the sorts of questions we have. Keep up the good work " – says, A.R.Norman from Oxford.

Now, try the Guide for yourself and add your opinion to those of the satisfied travellers to the South of Europe. Will your comments match theirs? Let it be known, regardless.

Address for your correspondence:

Karol Libura,
Le Guide Publications,
Spencer Close,
Park Royal,
London NW10 7DU.

INTRODUCTION

To reach your destination in France by car, the motorway w
certainly be the best alternative despite the tolls which will b
to a certain extent, offset by the steady saving on petr
consumption. You will find that it is a pleasure to rememb
picnicking in the Rest Areas which provide good facilitie
normally in splendid weather, thus adding to the safety of th
journey. And the scenery is frequently stunning and changi
all the way. For the first time comers it could be found qu
exotic, and it is. Besides the motorway is many times saf
than any other route.

The Guide presents its contents in a self-explanatory mann
as you progress your journey along the motorways covere
by this guide. The core of the guide consists of page
diagrammatically showing the motorway and the semicircul
"greens" as Rest Areas.

Petrol stations, hotels and restaurants are marked by the sic
of the Rest Areas at which the services are offered. The petr
stations are marked by a symbolic petrol pump, and similarl
the hotels and places of eating are indicated by a bed and
fork with a knife respectively.

Wherever it is appropriate, the hotels are cross-reference
with the page, on which the extended details are describe
including a photograph and a small map, side by side.

A number in black, between the Rest Areas, shows th
distance between them (km).

The distance between petrol stations, usually offering wic
range of services, is shown by a black number in a circle.

The number in red by the semi-circular "greens" indicates th
cumulative distance from the begining of your journey on th
motorway.

A red number in a red circle, at the top or bottom of the pag
(depending on the direction of travel), shows each page
total distance covered.

parallel to the diagrammatically shown motorway, there are rectangles on the opposite page which contain the names of the Rest Areas, symbols of the type of services offered, and a sentence or two of description relevant to the particular Area.

In this guide, all the accessible pull-ins allowing for a break in the journey, are called "REST AREAS", regardless of the type of services provided. But you may come across names like; service area, toll area or toll station.

It has to be said at this stage that almost all of the Rest Areas are attractive in their own ways, and there is always an Area within a short drive which should meet your particular needs.

Please note, that in this edition, some Rest Areas are noted as "lit at night" and some others are not. Some of the latter may well be lit.

And again, at some Rest Areas along the motorway the Info-Route service is provided but not all of them are specified in this edition.

On the small map of France with the relevant motorways marked on it, appearing at the top of every page showing the routes, there is a RED DOT which is represented by the content of the page, and the location of the DOT indicates your position on the motorway, along which you are travelling

The red arrow shows the direction of travel.

And finally, the Guide provides you with the information regarding the motorway, the toll, telephoning in France, hotels, diagrams allowing for efficient planning of your journey, translation of most of the French phrases appearing by the side of your motorway or elsewhere, that you would almost certainly like to understand, and some tips that you may find useful and a lot more besides.

THE TOLL

The toll is charged on the French motorway network except on sections in the immediate vicinity of towns.

At the entry to the charged sections of the motorways (Barrière de Péage) a ticket is normally obtainable from an automatic dispenser after pressing a button or it will be handed to you by an assistant. Fully automatic entries were introduced in 1987 where by stopping at the red light a ticket appears automatically in a slot which you must collect to change red light to green. The ticket gives information regarding the toll charges for all exits, depending on the category of the vehicle and the distance travelled.

At the exit "Barrière de Péage", the toll charge is normall paid to an assistant but at some locations there is, as wel an alternative way of paying, which is by throwing into "basket" the required amount in the right coins, about whic the information is given well in advance.

A separate marked lane must be used if change is require at locations where there is an automatic service. It is almos a "must" to have sufficient local currency.

The toll prices shown throughout the Guide are for passenge cars and they may be revised slightly during the year. Highe prices are payable for cars with caravans and for other typ of vehicles.

In order to get a receipt for payment at the exit "Barrière d Péage", you ask for a "Certificate de passage" or you pres a button to get one when using an automatic service lane

TELEPHONING

Since 25th October 1985, there have been changes introduce and they are as follows:-

There are now 2 telephone zones;

— PROVINCE and,
— PARIS/REGION PARISIENNE

All telephone numbers are of 8 figures.

For the PROVINCE, to the old 6 or 7 figure telephone numbe the Area Code numbers is added at the front accordingly

For the PARIS/REGION PARISIENNE zone:

— Paris,
— Hauts-de-seine,
— Siene-Saint-Denis,
— Val-de-Marne, a figure 4 is added at the front to the existin telephone number,

— Val-d'Oise, ·
— Yvelines, a figure 3 is added in a similar manner, and finally

— Essonne,
— Seine,
— Marne, a figure 6 is added at the front as above.

Note the following:

If the intended telephone — call receiver lives near the border of the two, previously neighbouring telephone areas, the Area Code of one or the other may be applicable.

So, if direct dialling is possible, you telephone:

To France from the UK;

1. To Paris/Region Parisienne, dial:
   010 33 1 (telephone number),

2. To the Province zone, dial:
   010 33 (telephone number).

From France to the UK, dial;

— 19,
— wait for the dialling tone, then dial:
— the Country Code (44),
— the Telephone Area Code (STD), minus the first zero,
— the telephone number.

An example to call London:
19 (wait) 44 1 961 1656

In France;

1. Within the PROVINCE ZONE;

— dial, just the 8 figure telephone number.

2. Within PARIS/REGION PARISIENNE ZONE;

— dial, just the 8 figure telephone number.

3. From PARIS/REGION PARISIENNE to
   the PROVINCE ZONE;

— dial 16,
— wait for dialling tone,
— dial the telephone number.

4. From the PROVINCE ZONE to
   the PARIS/REGION PARISIENNE ZONE:

— dial 16,
— wait for dialling tone,
— dial 1,
— dial the telephone number.

SYMBOLS

WC — WC, serves the purpose

 — WC with full facilities

 — Telephone

 — Handicapped facilities

 — Restaurant

 — Hotel

 — Shop

 — Cafeteria

 — Nursery

 — Currency exchange

 — Apparatus for children

 — Information

 — Post

Gend — Gendarmerie

SOS — Road side emergency telephone

ˉHE HOTELS

ˉhe hotels appearing in this publication, offer a full range of
ɥuality accommodation and relevant services, starting from
 to 4-star luxury hotels.

ˉhe hotels listed along the diagrams on pages 14 — 21, at
ʰe locations marked; "Aire de ....." are situated actually on
ʰe Rest Areas of the motorway, so you are not likely to be
ⁿconvenienced in any way. But to take advantage of the
ɛervices provided by the other hotels mentioned along the
ɖiagrams,it is necessary to leave the motorway. However, the
ɔcations of some of these hotels are just by the side of the
ɱotorway or very close by and may well be considered as
ɛqually convenient. Please,consult the relevant location map.

ᴀs you progress the journey along the actual routes of the
ɡuide you will see that the same is marked by diagrammatical
ɵeds; bigger bed which is shown on the left hand side of the
ɵoute, indicates hotel facilities at the Rest Areas, whereas the
ɵff-the-autoroute hotels are marked by the smaller bed
ɑppearing by the exit slip-roads where appropriate. With
ɛgard to the Pullman and some of the Altea hotels shown
ⁿ this guide,and in order to avoid repeating the long list of
ʰe high quality services offered, you need to take note of the
ɔllowing,in addition to the specific details of a particular
ʰotel;-

 Inter-hotel reservation ● fully equipped bathrooms ●
ɑutomatic morning call ● mini-bar ● radio ● television ●
ʟaundry and dry cleaning ● safes ● telex ● currency
ɛxchange● travel and entertainment reservation ● children
ɥp to 12 years of age are accepted free in the parent's room.

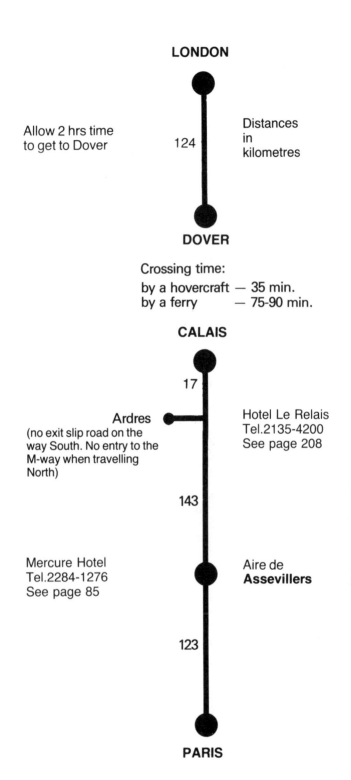

LONDON

Allow 2 hrs time to get to Dover

124

Distances in kilometres

DOVER

Crossing time:
by a hovercraft — 35 min.
by a ferry   — 75-90 min.

CALAIS

17

Ardres
(no exit slip road on the way South. No entry to the M-way when travelling North)

Hotel Le Relais
Tel.2135-4200
See page 208

143

Mercure Hotel
Tel.2284-1276
See page 85

Aire de
Assevillers

123

PARIS

The details of hotels in Paris are shown on pages 68-74

Hotel ARCADE, Portsmouth, - page 103
Hotel Novotel, Bayeux - page 230
Hotel Mercure, Caen - page 230

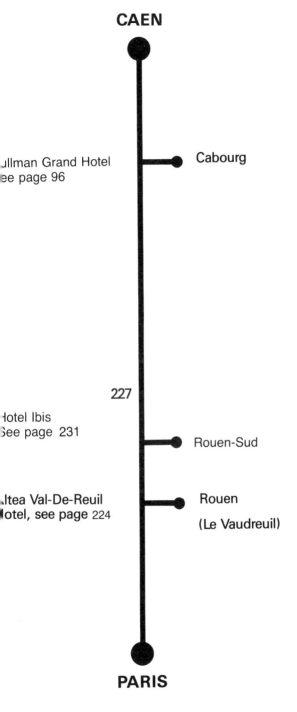

CAEN

ullman Grand Hotel
ee page 96

Cabourg

227

Hotel Ibis
See page 231

Rouen-Sud

ltea Val-De-Reuil
Hotel, see page 224

Rouen

(Le Vaudreuil)

PARIS

he details of hotels in Paris are shown on pages 68-74

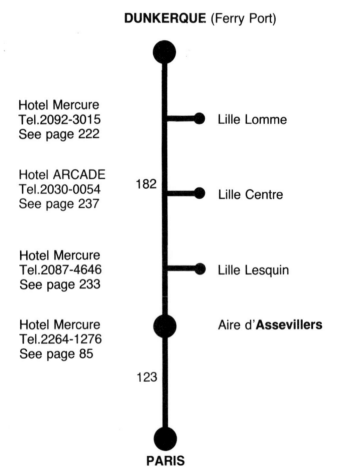

LONDON (Vauxhall Bridge)

Allow 2 hrs time to get to Ramsgate | 121 | Distances in kilometres

RAMSGATE

Crossing time = 150 min of experience with Sally Ferries, see page 166

DUNKERQUE (Ferry Port)

Hotel Mercure
Tel.2092-3015
See page 222

Lille Lomme

Hotel ARCADE
Tel.2030-0054
See page 237

182

Lille Centre

Hotel Mercure
Tel.2087-4646
See page 233

Lille Lesquin

Hotel Mercure
Tel.2264-1276
See page 85

Aire d'**Assevillers**

123

PARIS

The details of hotels in Paris are shown on pages 68-74

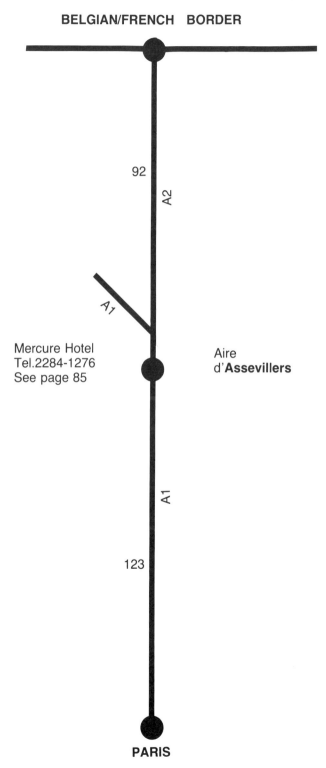

BELGIAN/FRENCH BORDER

92

A2

A1

Mercure Hotel
Tel.2284-1276
See page 85

Aire
d'**Assevillers**

A1

123

PARIS

he details of hotels in Paris are shown on pages 68-74

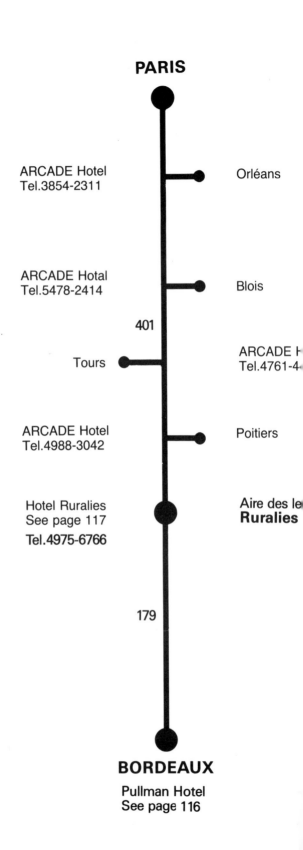

PARIS

ARCADE Hotel
Tel.3854-2311

Orléans

ARCADE Hotal
Tel.5478-2414

Blois

401

Tours

ARCADE H
Tel.4761-4

ARCADE Hotel
Tel.4988-3042

Poitiers

Hotel Ruralies
See page 117
Tel.4975-6766

Aire des le
Ruralies

179

BORDEAUX

Pullman Hotel
See page 116

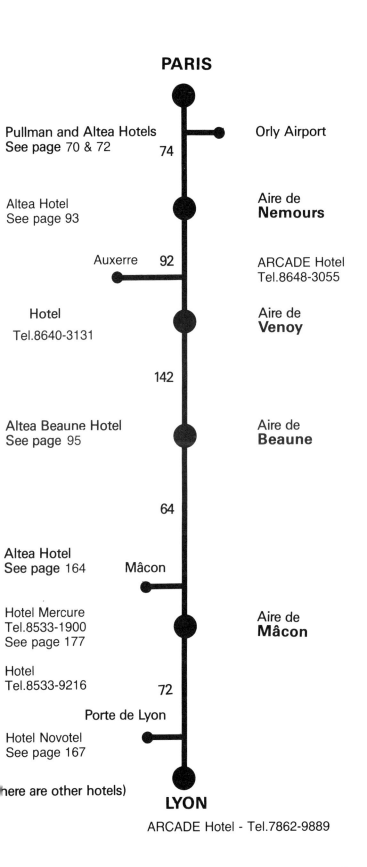

PARIS

Pullman and Altea Hotels
See page 70 & 72

74

Orly Airport

Altea Hotel
See page 93

Aire de
Nemours

Auxerre 92

ARCADE Hotel
Tel.8648-3055

Hotel
Tel.8640-3131

Aire de
Venoy

142

Altea Beaune Hotel
See page 95

Aire de
Beaune

64

Altea Hotel
See page 164

Mâcon

Hotel Mercure
Tel.8533-1900
See page 177

Aire de
Mâcon

Hotel
Tel.8533-9216

72

Porte de Lyon

Hotel Novotel
See page 167

here are other hotels)

LYON

ARCADE Hotel - Tel.7862-9889

19

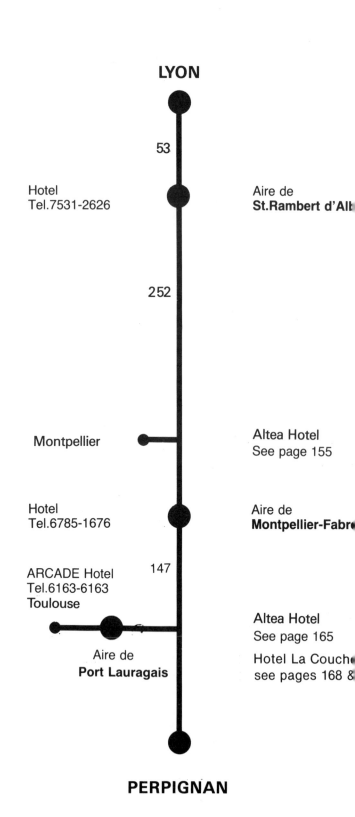

LYON

53

Hotel
Tel.7531-2626

Aire de
St.Rambert d'Alb

252

Montpellier

Altea Hotel
See page 155

Hotel
Tel.6785-1676

Aire de
Montpellier-Fabre

ARCADE Hotel
Tel.6163-6163
Toulouse

147

Altea Hotel
See page 165

Aire de
Port Lauragais

Hotel La Couch
see pages 168 &

PERPIGNAN

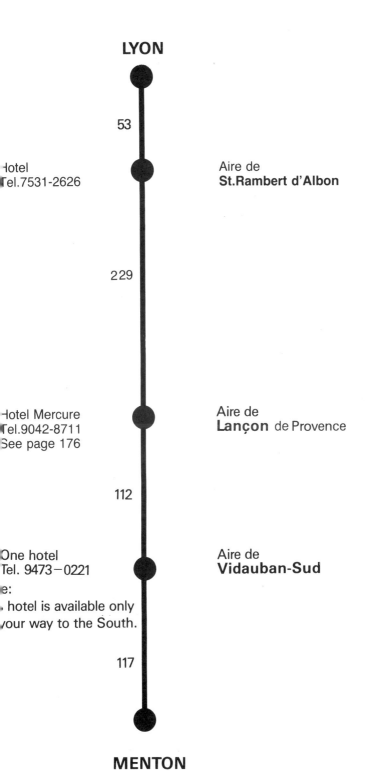

LYON

53

Hotel
Tel.7531-2626

Aire de
St.Rambert d'Albon

229

Hotel Mercure
Tel.9042-8711
See page 176

Aire de
Lançon de Provence

112

One hotel
Tel. 9473−0221
e:
 hotel is available only
your way to the South.

Aire de
Vidauban-Sud

117

MENTON

For hotels of the Riviera and along the Coast,
see pages 148 - 155.

YOUR CHECK-LIST

1. Full driving licence,

2. Car registration document and written authority for us if the car is not in your name,

3. Breakdown insurance cover, well appreciated when yc do, require help ,

4. Your tickets,

5. Passport. Must be valid beyond the date of return,

6. Money, travellers cheques. Cheque book, credit card — keep them separately,

7. Green Card — no longer compulsory in France, eve with the British third party insurance, which gives yc better cover than the minimum otherwise applying France. However,a fully comprehensive insurance advisable.

8. G B sticker — for Great Britain,

9. Red triangle. Compulsory for France if your car is n equipped with hazard warning lights. Recommende in any case.

10. Spare set of light bulbs, a "must",

11. Main beam deflector. You no longer need to have yello tinted lenses,

12. First aid kit,

13. Fire extinguisher,

14. Petrol can (Must be empty on ferries),

15. Basic tools, including feeler gauge,

16. Spare parts; e.g. plugs,points,hoses,fan belt ...

17. Driving glasses, of course,

18. 2-pin plug adaptor for your electrical equipment,

19. Michelin Map of Paris (blue cover — 100 metres to 1 cn a "must" if you contemplate driving into Paris.

WHY IS IT BIG ENDS ALWAYS GO N LITTLE PLACES LIKE LE BROCQ?

On a recent family motoring holiday in France, Mr. John Attenborough's car had a breakdown. "A major breakdown," in his own words. The car's big end had gone.

It was on the border with Spain, in the foothills of the Pyrenees. The holiday could have been in ruins, had he not taken out the AA's 5-Star Service.

Mr. Attenborough made one call to the AA's Emergency Centre in Boulogne. Within hours, he was continuing his journey in a hire car paid for by the AA (his own car was brought home for him).

On his return journey, he left the hire car at St. Malo, and was met by a Hertz representative at Portsmouth with a brand new car to get him home.

AA's 5-Star Service will cover your car, your family, against sickness or illness, and your belongings.

All for the price of a family meal.

INTRODUCTION TO L'ARCHE'S RESTAURANTS

L'Arche is a respected brand name for a major chain c restaurants covering the motorway network in France an offering a relaxing stopover at relevant Rest Areas, which ar marked by L'Arches logo throughout this guide.

L'Arche restaurants will provide you with reasonably price meals or snacks,all year round,from 7.00 a.m. — 10.30 p.m (at least). The absolute cleanliness of L'Arche restaurant including the kitchens, so obviously backed by kind an courteous staff, inspires total confidence.

So do not be surprised to find perfectly kept lavatories or telephone in good working order. C'est normal.

Further more, L 'Arche offers you; a ''Baby's Corner'', a pla ground for children, and a selected range of sweets an biscuits.

And finally, see pages 82 and 83 for an at — a — glance ma showing the locations of L'Arche's restaurants in France. A you know, since L'Arche is the biggest company in th catering business, it would be desirable to hear your opinion and comments, in order that the restaurants can maintain the high standard of service.

In conclusion; kindness,courtesy and quality is exactly wha L'Arche's restaurants have at their disposal, and are eager t serve you with.

(write to the address shown under ''Look no further'')

WE ARE NUMBER ONE

The British Press, including the professionals from motor and caravan magazines, have reviewed the guide very favourably, and seem to have confirmed the assumption that the "Le Guide" has already become The Number One guide book for the independent motorway traveller in France. But the most important of all are the comments from the very users of the guide, expressed to me, in letters and personal conversations, during my frequent trips to France.

Your letters continue to confirm the unequivocal support for the publication which undoubtedly fuels further development of the guide. Here are some quotes which I cannot resist the temptation of sharing;-

Last year I used your guide, Motorway to the Sun (France) and found it invaluable in my travels. I would like to purchase the latest updated version (mine is 1986) for my trip this year. My only criticism of the book was, it fell apart very quickly and had loads of loose pages" - says, June Hare from Worcester Park in Surrey. (Ed. Poor binding of first edition now resolved)

Mr.W.H.Searle from Twyford, Reading; "I bought my first Le Guide (which fell to bits) in the departure lounge at Hoverspeed Dover, quite literally as I was dashing out for my flight. On the journey down I thanked my lucky stars that I had spotted the guide on the stand just in time, before leaving. What a Godsend."

And finally, from Dorothy Skelly, Bessacarr, Doncaster; "My family bought your book before travelling through France to Nimes last summer. We were delighted by its accuracy and usefulness. Once again, thank you for your excellent publication".

KINDNESS, COURTESY, QUALITY

As you know, the last edition; Autoroutes to the Sun, was followed up by the issue of circular stickers which have been displayed along the relevant motorways in France and elswhere to indicate, not only good quality service where appropriate, but the kindness and courtesy which goes with it, thus, bringing satisfaction to the proprietors and the users of the Guide.

Establishments of interest to the users of Le Guide vary in quality from "very good" to "excellent", all show the same sign of Le Guide. In order to do justice in covering the range of high quality service, a variation to the design of stickers has been produced and from now on you will come across plain signs of Le Guide and ones bearing the words "Excellence and Quality", as shown on page 84.

The plain signs of Le Guide are displayed at places where the available service is of relevant quality and sometimes the value for money governs the decision. But in all cases the cleanliness is looked at, first. The plain logos are shown as well at places which sell the guide book.

I would like you to know that there have been occasional cases of disparity in the quality of service and the stickers were removed, in order to avoid possible disappointments to travellers.

If you wish to display the logo on your car, bearing in mind its implication; *KINDNESS, COURTESY, QUALITY,* you will be posted one, free of charge upon request. There are Le Guide stickers for inside use on glass and for outside use on glass or car body. They are 90 mm in diameter.

THE SAFETY OF DRIVING

I found it a compelling obligation to give the subject some prominence wherever possible due to the seriousness of the topic. I have no doubt that Le Guide will persuade many of its users to take the basics of safety with proper understanding thus reducing the trend in the rising number of accidents.

And, I hope to be forgiven for having approved some pages of the guide saturated with depressing news which imply warning, warning and warning.

But when you witness the everyday madness of keeping too close to the vehicle in front which overrides many other safety precautions, you will understand.

The focus of public attention must be on safe driving speed and fatigue in particular, to safeguard better prospects for enjoying super holidays in the years to come, built on experience of the past.

THE POWER FACTOR OF LE GUIDE

Oh yes. With the growing popularity of the LE GUIDE book due to its comprehensiveness and quality of information followed up by the issue of stickers, we are talking about growing numbers of people involved: namely, the independent motorway travellers in France, as far as this particular guide is concerned, as other guides are in the pipeline e.g. Ostende - West Berlin.

he sustained growth of Le Guide users, represents the ower which can and should be used, in order to maintain, or btain the required quality of service while on the route. And, ue to competition of companies fighting for our monies, it hould be very easy to put effective pressure and favour the nes that we approve of, or ignore the ones of which we isapprove. So, if you care, let your comments be known and hrough Le Guide we can achieve, the otherwise unachievble.

ear in mind that Le Guide is on sale in France and the orthern countries of Europe, too. Thus, the wishes of the Le uide members, so to speak, cannot afford to be ignored.

or the benefit of all Le Guide members, please, share what ou think is worth sharing. Tell the story of your holiday; good, ad, funny or ridiculous so as to warn, learn, laugh and have a ood time. Recommend your holiday place, a good garage, lace of interest, anything and everything. Let's be useful to ach other, there will not be a better way. Unless, of course; ou know different, as the famous Esther says. Tell us.

ICKING-UP A PARKING FOR YOUR PICNIC

s you may know, there is always a Rest Area within a short rive that will suit your particular needs and whichever Rest rea you select prior to pulling-in, you may find it helpful to hark in the Guide your own detailed description of the Area or future reference, as no doubt, you will drive the same route gain.

a selection of a Rest Area is to be made for staying vernight, make sure that safety is looked at, first. You would e considered "brave" to stay on your own, however, the ther extreme could be, unwittingly joining a bunch of ndesirables, unknowingly.

happened to me personally at the end of one summer. On ny own, I was cruising along the Autoroute du Soleil, I was red, it was getting late and I wanted to make a break in my ourney. At random, I picked up a very pretty Rest Area which appened to be deserted at the time. I parked my car away om the filling station complex, hoping perhaps for a nap on he nearby bench which I soon found to be very comfortable.

fter a while a scruffy looking car pulled in, some 20 metres way and located itself distinctly towards the exit from the rea, which somehow alerted my attention. Two human-like reatures left the car and disappeared in the shadow of trees. ly shiny car's front door was left wide open and at that articular time I was doing my best impression of the Sleeping eauty.

Soon, a shadow emerged from the scruffy car which
managed to identify, not without difficulty, to be of a female
Visibly she seemed to be attracted by what I considered to b
my territory for the moment. I began to sense trouble afoot

Suddenly, I remembered a story about a case in which
woman attacked a man, yelling at the same time for hel
which was obviously available immediately. When the "help
arrived the man was robbed. A carbon copy of what had bee
taking place, so far. At that time I lost interest in the furthe
development of what might have been a good story to repor

I suddenly found that I had felt, quite all right, and hurriedl
continued my journey.

THE AA'S 5-STAR SERVICE

My latest trip to the Continent was interrupted by a majc
breakdown of my car which took place on January 8th 1989.
just managed to leave the A26 - L'Autoroute des Anglais (th
French call it L'Autoroute du Nord) at Calais and had to com
to a halt at the very end of the exit slip road, leading to th
local road network. I hardly managed to establish the degre
of the breakdown when an Englishman - a complete strange
driving a French registered car, pulled in and offered hel
which was a kind gesture in the circumstances, though
nothing could have been done on the spot.

My new English colleague was very helpful indeed. He wer
out of his way to telephone the AA's 5-Star Service a
Boulogne and came back to confirm that help was on the wa
and should be with me within half an hour. Whilst waiting fc
the arrival of the breakdown patrol, many drivers, English an
French offered help which I found extremely encouraging.
noticed that many of the cars displayed the LE GUIDE sticke
and I wonder whether it had anything to do with the fact that
too, had my LE GUIDE sign shown on my car's rear window

Anyway, the 5-Star breakdown agent arrived sooner tha
expected. The area of my breakdown spot was marked b
traffic cones for safety reasons and within 20 minutes my ca
and the other 2 members of my party were on the way t
Calais Port. My car was unloaded onto a deck of The Pride c
Dover and soon we enjoyed a meal on the ferry as if nothin
had happened.

At Dover my car was towed through passport and custom
control points and left with the AA. With little delay my car an
the party were on the way home in full comfort of th
purposely designed, spacious cabin of the AA's Relay Servic
vehicle. I hope that all members of the AA's recovery servic
are as kind as the one whom we had the pleasure of bein
looked after.

have been a member of the AA for 18 years and I urge the users of this guide to arrange an insurance which will provide help when it is required and the AA's 5-Star Service cover seems to be the obvious choice, at least we know how good they are. Do not even contemplate going abroad without the cover. (No, I am not an agent of The Automobile Association !)

And finally, I would like to thank very much all my fellow travellers for offering me help and especially the anonymous Englishman who came from nowhere and went away as anonymously as he had come. I repeat, myself here; let's be useful to each other, let's follow the fine example of the anonymous Englishman.

One feels great to be in such good company.

STOP PRESS

The Arcade chain of hotels gives 10% on the price of accommodation upon presentation of a copy of LE GUIDE. However, this offer does not cover hotels in Paris and airports.

THE BASICS ON FRENCH WINES

(extracts from the work of Sally Brompton, permitted to appear in Le Guide by the copyright holders; Eveldon Press)

There is more pretentious clap-trap talked about wine than any other drink in the world. The fact is that most of us really could not care less whether a wine is a little cheeky or downright insulting. What we want to know is whether it is red or white, dry or sweet, still or sparkling, delicious or disgusting.

One point to remember when choosing French wines is that they are graded by law into four main categories. In descending order these are:

Appellation Controlee (AC),
Vins Delimite de Qualite Superieure (VDQS),
Vins de Pays,
Vins de Table.

AC wines are the best and, generally speaking, the more specific the appellation, the better the wine. So a named vineyard is more important than a village, followed by an area and, finally, a region.

The vintages are intended only as a guide. A good year depends on the climate but there are always a few poor wines produced in a vintage year while the occasional fine wine can slip through in an otherwise bad year.

Forget everything you have ever read about the "right" glass for a particular wine. For normal drinking any glass will do for any wine - the bigger, the better, but leave your wine space to breathe by filling the glass no more than half-way.

But if you are drinking wine with a meal, avoid vinegar and lemon as they tend to make the wine taste sour.

WHITE WINE

As the ideal, anytime, all-round drink, white wine takes a lot of beating. It can adapt to any situation, whether it is the kind of celebration that calls for a bottle of Champagne, or a glass of dry white in your local pub. It goes with food or without it, is equally at home as an aperitif, or a long drink - mixed with ice and soda, to quench the fiercest summer thirst. It can be sweet or dry, still or sparkling, light or heavy and, of course good or bad.

White wine should be chilled before drinking and the cheaper or sweeter the wine the colder it generally needs to be. Do not stick the bottle in the freezer which can kill the flavour and - if you are forgetful - turn the wine into ice-lollies.

Unlike red wines, white wines are normally drunk when they are young, although some of the better ones will improve with keeping-especially the sweet dessert wines such as Sauternes.

As far as food is concerned white wine goes with pretty well everything. It is probably at its best with fish and poultry but if you want to drink it with roast beef-go right ahead. A few of the really sweet wines are better by themselves or with a simple fresh fruit dessert. But, there again, it is all a matter of taste.

Champagne certainly does not need food with it although there are people who will drink it happily all the way through a meal.

RED WINE

Red wine is normally dry and should, ideally, be served at room temperature which means opening it an hour or two before pouring it. It can be sipped or quaffed, drunk by itself or with food, and goes with pretty well everything except fish which is nothing to do with etiquette but the fact that red wines tend to make the fish taste metallic.

Rose wine can be sweet or dry, still or sparkling, should always be served chilled and can be drunk at any time. But do not waste good food on it.

And, talking of food, while you cannot really go far wrong drinking your favourite wine with your favourite meal, there are a few simple rules you may want to keep in mind.

Firstly, good food deserves good wine so if you are having roast beef pick the best wine you can afford. Peasant foods such as spaghetti bolognaise or shepherd's pie call for something cheap and cheerful. Blander foods such as chicken and ham go with lighter wines such as Beaujolais. While rich dishes like oxtail need something hearty like a Burgundy. All cheeses go splendidly with wine but the milder ones best with heavier, more mature wines while strong flavours like Roquefort take something younger and lighter.

And do not be ashamed to order the house wine when you are out. It is often better than most of the alternatives at the lower - sometimes even the middle - part of the list. It makes sense since the proprietor is probably getting a better deal by buying it in bulk.

Finally, remember that when it comes down to the nitty-gritty, the most important thing about any wine is whether you enjoy it. The best wine in the world is worthless if you, personally, do not like it.

So do not be intimidated by the know-alls who try to impress you with their copy-book opinions of what is good and what is not.

CHEERS!

DID YOU KNOW THAT . . .

. . . incorrect tyres pressure and in particular those below the specified recommendation, have been attributable to many serious accidents. Pressures should be checked frequently. One comment here; since the recommended tyre pressure is for cold tyres you would be expected to add about 3-4 lb/in² (0.3 kg/cm²) if topping-up becomes necessary when the tyre is hot.

It is important to understand that when a tyre is under-inflated, rubber fatigue is taking place which results from repeated tyre deflections. And when you consider a case of a speed 80 mph (about 130 km/h), the tyre deflects about 20 times in one second.

The heat which is obviously generated in the process adds to the gravity of the problem, especially during the summer time when the ambiant temperature is high. Needless to say, the ultimate stage is bursting of the tyre. One could go on further still; with under-inflated tyres there is a further danger of difficult road holding, especially when negotiating bends.

With correct tyres pressure you are likely to find an improvement in fuel consumption.

Never drive with under-inflated tyres.

... according to my research exercise it seems to be apparent that about 55% of motorists underestimate the braking distance as a function of speed at normal conditions. 25% show a complete ignorance, ugh... 20% proudly boast, just about right.

Very few motorists were able to elaborate on the topic. See page 36 showing graphs from which you will get the message at a glance. Memorise the graphs.

• • • driving at a speed of 80 mph (about 130 km/h) you travel 40 yards in one second. So, when you need to bring your car to halt, you will require at least 0.7 of a second to process your requirement and react by pressing the brake pedal. By then your car will have travelled 28 yards and the actual braking process begins to be effective, obviously, subject to the condition of the braking system of your car.

And now, the braking distance would vary, depending on road conditions. But, if you brake too hard, your car may lose "contact" with the road surface and you skid. And when the skidding stage is reached, you are in grave danger yourself and put others into the same rotten boat, against their will. It would not be fair. Be realistic, KEEP YOUR DISTANCE.

• • • in Sweden you are not allowed any content of alcohol in your blood stream.

Alcohol in your blood stream is a killer, number 2, following fatigue. The obvious risk of an accident lies in a false sense of confidence which comes with drinking, and therefore, the false ability to drive cannot match the real requirements of the road.

• • • fatigue, which normally follows lack of rest and monotonous driving, is the main cause of accidents involving death. And if you consider that 90% of information which is

ecessary to drive a motorvehicle comes through what you
ee (vision) then you may become a bit more sympathetic to
e problem and fight fatigue by taking frequent breaks during
ur travels. Experience tells that one may get some help
om listening to the radio. Have your cassettes ready for use
hen on the road. Prepare them the day before you travel.

. . the circulation system of an average adult contains about
) pints (5.68 litres) of blood. Each drop is made up of 250
illion red cells, 400,000 white cells and 15 million smaller
atelets suspended in a clear yellowish fluid called plasma.
ven when you are resting, each drop of blood passes
rough the heart and lungs once every minute - up to 8 times
minute during stress and exertion. Red cells carry oxygen
om the lungs to all body tissues. White cells fight invading
erms. Platelets help the blood to clot. Plasma carries not
lly these cells but also many vital chemical substances. It
so contains "antibodies" which help in the defence against
vaders, and other substances which help stop bleeding.
.d. printed after the Department of Health and Social Security and
e Central Office of Information 1982)

OTORWAY DESIGN AND USAGE AS
AUSES OF BEHAVIOURAL PROBLEMS
MONG DRIVERS

Dr.Ivan D.Brown (Ed.Extracts)

otorways have improved mobility and safety in the road
ansport system. However, their safety relative to other roads
 often overstated: drivers are propably only 50% safer on
otorways, compared with non-build-up A roads. Most
otorway accidents are attributed to 'errors' in driving
ehaviour, such as speeding, close following, poor lane
scipline and failure to adapt to adverse conditions. Some of
ese problems undoubtedly result from recklessness and
arelessness.

owever, there is evidence suggesting that the design and
ormal use of motorways can be a contributory factor in
ccidents. Their relatively featureless nature poses problems
r the perception of speed and distance, the judgement of
afety margins and, particularly, the maintenance of alert-
ess. Continuous high-speed driving causes speed to be
nderestimated and, in heavy traffic, contributes to speed
ress effects. All these problems are exacerbated among
rofessional drivers working irregular hours and suffering
om sleep disruption.

Behavioural problems of this kind are presented as the natur response of human brain when driving is prolonged in motorway environment.

Motorways are a necessary development in high-speed roa transport, if society is to balance its increasing requiremen for mobility and safety. Mobility has certainly been enormou ly improved by the introduction of relatively straight a well-surfaced multi-lane roads, with hard shoulders, opposing traffic streams, no crossing traffic, no pedestrian cyclists, or learners, and clear route information. In theor this reduction in demand on drivers should also ha improved safety, and of course it has. The casualty rate motorways has gone down to less than one-seventh that the casualty rate in the road system as a whole (Dept. Transport, 1986).

However, exception must be taken to the repeated asserti (e.g. see Dept.of Transport, 1987) that motorways are times safer than other roads". This claim is spurious. Safety a function of usage and relative safety can therefore expressed validly only if it involves comparisons of simil user groups. The higher accident rate on 'other road involves numerous road users who are not legally permitted use motorways. Thus, vehicle occupants are not 8 times saf on motorways than they would be on other roads! Th comparison of motorways with 'other roads' is also of litt significance for transport authorities, because it contras parts of the systems serving quite different functions.

Using a more legitimate and meaningful comparison alternative routes for powered vehicles, we find that mot ways are only three times as 'safe' as non-built-up A roa (Dept. of Transport, 1986, p.71). They are only twice as sa when road works are in evidence (Dept. of Transport, 198 p.27).

An even more relevant comparison, for my present propos is between driver safety on motorways and reasonat alternative non-motorway routes. The total number of casu ties is about equal for car drivers and motor vehic passengers (87, 302 vs 81846, Dept. of Transport, 198 p.111). Therefore, at a rough estimate, the 3:1 safety benef of motorway travel compared with non-built-up A roads m actually reduce to only a 50% safety advantage for motorw drivers.

This is highly important for any consideration of behaviou problems among motorway drivers. Drivers' behaviour determined partly by what they believe about safety. If th are told that "motorways are 8 times safer than other road and they believe this to mean that driving is 8 times saf when in fact it may be only 1 & 1/2 times safer than on an alternative route, they may be encouraged to behave far more riskily than traffic situations actually demand. Spurious claims for the benefits of motorways are thus likely to be counterproductive for road safety.

Fortunately, in this respect, driver behaviour is determined more by their own perceptions of risk and safety in traffic situations than by what they are told about objective safety. Unfortunately, however, risk perception depends upon two somewhat unreliable factors:

. drivers' indentification and evaluation of potential hazards in traffic and,

. their belief in their ability to deal with traffic hazards.

There is evidence that most drivers think they are safer and more skilled than the average motorist, which is clearly impossible.

This overrating of their own abilities may lead drivers into taking risks they cannot handle adequately, which suggests that driver training and education have more of a role to play in road safety than we have been prepared to accept so far, in this country (Ed.Great Britain). More importantly, in the present context, is the evidence from laboratory and field studies showing that factors common in motorway driving can actually impair drivers' ability to identify and evaluate traffic hazards appropriately.

The aims of this paper are to outline the nature of such behavioural problems and the types of appropriate remedial measure that could reduce their contribution to accidents.

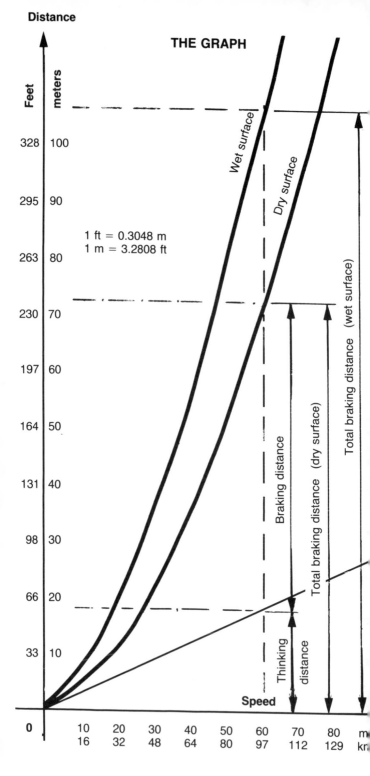

The diagram shows the minimum stopping distance a
function of speed at normal conditions; alert driver,
ground, good braking system of your car, good tyres.

MEDICAL MATTERS OF RELEVANCE

(Ed. Extracts from Papers of Dr. IVAN D. BROWN from Medical Research Council, Applied Psychology Unit, Cambridge, permitted to appear in LE GUIDE by the copyright holders The Medical Commission on Accident Prevention)

FATIGUE

What is Fatigue ?

Most people would have little difficulty in answering this question. Their answers would almost certainly imply that fatigue is what they experience after a prolonged period of work: an increasing disinclination to continue performing the task in hand, accompanied by general and localised aches and pains, the nature of which depends to some extent on what they have been doing. Subjectively, this experience seems to be the output of a feedback mechanism which prevents the body over-exerting itself. Pressed harder, some people might find it more difficult to explain why fatigue is sometimes experienced when they have been working for only a short time, whilst others may admit that they can feel fatigue merely thinking about work waiting to be done! Perhaps even more surprisingly, most people readily accept that fatigue symptoms often disappear completely when the work in hand is exchanged for some novel or more enjoyable activity.

CONCLUSIONS

(Ed. The following is the result of research on Medical Aspects of Fitness to Drive)

✓ Driving fatigue is not solely determined by the length of time spent at the wheel, although most individuals will experience some fatigue symptoms if driving is prolonged about four hours.

✓ Fatigue can be transferred to driving from prior manual or non-manual activity.

✓ In practice, fatigue from prolonged driving interacts with behavioural changes that result from normal diurnal variations in physiological activity. These factors combine to maximis[e] adverse effects of fatigue when driving extends into th[e] normal sleeping hours of the individual.

d/ Sleep loss and degradation in sleep quality which resu[lt] from irregular driving schedules seriously exacerbate effec[ts] of driving fatigue. Persistent irregular work-schedules ca[n] lead to chronic fatigue.

e/ Certain personality characteristics mediate the effects [of] driving fatigue. Extroversion seems to exacerbate thes[e] effects.

f/ Prolonged static muscular contraction is the prime cause [of] physiological fatigue in driving. Psychologically, the ma[in] dangers result from boredom when driving under fair[ly] undemanding environmental conditions and from the motiva[-] tional pressures to complete a journey for professional [or] social reasons.

g/ Individuals are normally sensitive to their state of fatigu[e.] Problems arise for road safety mainly when fatigued driver[s'] judgements are impaired by alcohol or illness, and whe[n] commercial or social pressures persuade them to override th[e] warning conveyed by their own fatigue symptoms.

ADVICE

a/ The seating in a vehicle should be comfortable, to ensur[e] good posture and stability with minimal static muscula[r] contraction. Dials should be clearly visible, without glare an[d] producing no disturbing reflections in the windscreen. A[ll] controls should be within easy reach. Seat adjustment[s] should be made to eliminate stretching or slumping, both [of] which restrict circulation. Postural changes which usuall[y] accompany aggressive driving, or attempts to maintai[n] unrealistic time schedules, will exacerbate static muscula[r] fatigue and should be avoided.

b/ The temperature and ventilation controls of the vehic[le] should permit the body to be comfortably warm while allowin[g] cool air to be directed to the face. Care should be taken tha[t] engine fumes and exhaust gases do not enter the car an[d] cause monoxide poisoning.

c/ A high noise level from the engine, or continuous wind roa[r] from open windows, is more likely to induce fatigue in the lon[g] run than an adequately ventilated car with closed window[s] and a quiet engine.

d/ It is inadvisable to undertake a long drive immediately afte[r] exhausting muscular activity.

Meals taken before and during a drive should not be heavy, the subsequent processes of digestion will induce sleepiness and difficulty in concentration.

Alcohol especially should be avoided before and during a long drive.
Even quite small amounts can disrupt the distribution of attention among task demands and larger quantities readily lead to drowsiness, inaccuracy and impaired judgement, whilst at the same time giving a false sense of confidence.

Many drugs in therapeutic doses can induce fatigue especially in the early stage of treatment, patients should be warned about this.

Driving demands a high order of concentration, which must be maintained for long periods of relative monotony when no particular need for attention is apparent. Regular rest periods are therefore desirable. Breaks of at least 20 minutes seem necessary if alertness is to be restored, although the effectiveness of rest periods in permitting recovery diminishes as driving is prolonged beyond four or five hours. Where the total driving period extends beyond about nine hours, breaks may produce negligible recovery of alertness.

If a driver feels physically uncomfortable he should stop the vehicle and take a short walk to relieve the adverse effects of static muscular contraction. Recovery from muscular fatigue is best achieved by frequent short breaks. If the driver feels drowsy, longer breaks, preferably including opportunities for sleep are indicated.

Regular rest pauses are more important where driving conditions are relatively undemanding of attention, such as on a motorway, or at night in light traffic, because alertness can fall dangerously low before the driver becomes aware of his impaired efficiency.

Drivers should avoid taking occasional long journeys which extend into that part of the 24 hours when they would normally be sleeping. Diurnal changes in physiological activation can combine with effects of prolonged driving to depress alertness drastically between midnight and 0600 hrs.

Drivers of an extreme extrovert personality seem particularly susceptible to fatigue under relatively unchanging environmental conditions. They should therefore take special note of the above environmental conditions.
The older driver (i.e. over 45 years) is also more susceptible to fatigue, recovers increasingly less completely from rest-pauses during prolonged driving, and is more adversely affected by irregular working hours.

m/ No drivers can afford to ignore, for long, subjective
experienced fatigue symptoms of discomfort, drowsiness
irritability. They should certainly take a break when fatigu
effects are detected in their driving performance, such a
mistimed gearchanges, unanticipated events, and nea
misses.

FATIGUE AND DRIVERS OF HEAVY GOODS VEHICLES
AND PUBLIC SERVICES VEHICLES

The above recommendations apply to all drivers, but th
following points should be emphasised:

a/ With the greater forces and more frequent control move
ments normally required in larger vehicles, there is a greate
need to ensure a good stable posture by taking full advantag
of any adjustments provided to the driving position. There
also a greater need to avoid the tense posture which usual
results from working under time stress.

b/ Much greater concentration and anticipation is require
with larger vehicles, because of their lower manoeuvrability.
is therefore particularly important to avoid taking alcohol an
heavy meals just before or during a work-spell, as these ar
known to impair anticipatory judgements and reduce aler
ness.

c/ Regular and frequent short rest-pauses permit efficien
recovery from muscular fatigue, but breaks of at last 2
minutes seem necessary to restore alertness. The effective
ness with which an acceptable level of arousal is recovere
declines with total time spent in driving. After about nin
hours, psychophysiological recovery is minimal, even afte
rest-pauses of 20 minutes or more.

d/ Shared driving which requires the off-duty driver to trav
and sleep on the vehicle produces more fatigue than that i
which sharing operates on a relay system, because both th
quality and quantity of sleep are likely to be impaired. A slee
debt may also be accumulated by sleeping in noisy condition
away from home.

e/ Drivers should aim for as regular a work-schedule a
possible, from one day to the next, with ample time (at leas
six hours) allowed for consecutive hours of sleep. Irregula
hours not only reduce the effectiveness of sleep, they ca

lso depress alertness by disrupting the physiological
hanges which the body normally undergoes each 24 hours
when more stable routines are worked. Irregular hours may
lso produce a cumulative sleep debt. Older drivers are
articularly susceptible to these adverse effects arising from
rolonged and irregular hours of work.

Legislators should aim to regulate the "duty hours" of
rofessional drivers, rather than their "driving time", if fatigue
ffects transferred from non-driving aspects of the job are to
e minimised. Regulations should tend to produce stable
work-schedules, which permit adequate periods of continuous
leep at regular times each day. Provision for mandatory
reaks during the "duty time" is essential, although there is
uch to be said for giving the individual driver some latitude
s to when, and for how long, he takes his daily allowance of
est breaks.

Employers should comply with the mandatory requirements
n drivers' hours of work and should minimise motivational
ressures on drivers to complete journeys when they are
onsciously aware of major fatigue symptoms.

XPRESSIONS OF THE ROUTE

ccôtement non stabilisé − *soft, hard shoulder*

llumez vos feux − *switch on your lights*

ttention, sortie de camions — *careful, lorries turning*

uberge de Jeunesse — *Youth hostel*

arrière de péage — *toll barrier*

ison Futé — *summer time operating, advisory service for
otorists*

ruit — *noise*

edez le passage − *give way*

entre Ville — *town centre*

ette cabine peut être appelée à ce numero − *this cabin may
e telephoned under this number ...*

Changeur de monnaie — *money exchange*

Chaussée déformée — *uneven, bad surface*

Danger vent — *dangerous wind*

Défense d'entrée — *entrance forbidden*

Déviation — *diversion*

Disque de stationnement — *Blue zone parking dis (obtainable in France from a Police station or Tourist office*

Douane — *customs*

Eau potable — *drinking water*

Essence (normale) — *2 star petrol*

Eteignez vos feux — *switch off your lights*

Fin d'allumage de feux – *switch off your lights*

Gravillons — *loose chippings (gravel)*

Hôtel de Ville — *Town Hall*

Halte à péage – *stop at the toll barrier*

Jeux, mis a la disposition des enfants aux risques et perils d utilisateurs — *utilisation of the apparatus should be unde supervision of parents*

Ni vitesse, ni bruit — *no speed, no noise*

Nids de poules — *potholes*

Parcours sportif adultes — *exercise track for adults*

Par la passerelle — *to the footbridge*

Passage protégé — *right of way*

Peage — *toll*

Pique-nique, jeux d'enfants — *picnic area, suitable for partie with young children*

Pièce acceptée — *coins accepted (usually appears befo approaching the barrier of toll)*

Pluie — *slippery (after raining)*

oids lourds — *heavy vehicles (normally associated with a road sign, showing a route to be followed)*

réparez votre monnaie — *have your coins ready*

riorité à droite — *priority of the traffic coming out of the right and side*

ropriété privée — *private property*

ainnuarage – *road longitudinally grooved (special notice to e taken by motorcyclists)*

appel — *reminding the last warning*

egardez votre distance de sécurité – *keep safe distance to e vehicle in fromt*

alentir – *slow*

isque de verglas — *black ice, icy patches*

oulez au pas — *dead slow*

alle à langer — *nursery facilities*

ans monnaie — *for those without coins (change)*
ans plomb – *Unleaded petrol*
auf riverains — *no entry except for access of inhabitants*

errez à droite — *keep to the right*

errez à gauche — *keep to the left*

yndicat d'Initiative — *Tourist Information Office*

ortie, (Sortie de voiture) — *exit*

ortie prochaine — *next exit*

tationnement interdit – *parking prohibited*

uper — *4 star petrol*

n train peut en cacher un autre — *one train hides another ne (on level crossing)*

outes directions — *all traffic*

ehicules lents, restez à votre droite — *slow vehicles, keep the right*

Verglas — *black ice, patches of ice.*

Verifiez votre monnaie — *check your change (coins)*

Vers — *towards (Vers Lyon)*

Vitesse — *speed*

Voir à droite — *look to the right*

Vous n'avez pas la priorité — *you have no right of way*

NN (Nouvelles Normes) — *new rating system for hotels*

Police de route or Garde Mobile — *Traffic Police Patrol*

TIPS PLUS

— Important, make sure that the braking system of your ca
is in order. Have it bled and the fluid changed if necessar

**Remember, high altitude driving in hot weather
may affect the efficiency of the braking system of
your car.**

— Have the tyres pressure right, check frequently.

— It is a good idea to begin your journey with the petrol tan
full.

— Drive on the right side of the road which happens on th
Continent to be the right hand side.

— **Be aware of the priority of traffic coming out fror
the right hand side.**

— "Passage protegé" — right of way. Ignore it, it can b
disastrous. Just drive with care.

— Keep your own pace and safe distance from the vehicl
in front.

— Do not drive between two heavy vehicles, do enjoy a goo
view all round. Besides, at the extremes you will not ge
sandwiched.

- On the main road be very careful.Some road users appearing at speed from your right hand side, may give you a bad headache.

- On the motorway, closer to the Italian border, there are sections of contra-flow traffic. Be careful, as in one case I found, (perhaps due to tiredness) your lane seems to disappear as if it was an exit slip road and you may be tempted, in confusion to drive straight on, against the oncoming traffic.

- At certain mountainous sections of the motorway, there is no "hard shoulder", but frequent SOS bays are provided instead.

- Seat belt rule, as in the UK. On the whole of the French road network,including the towns, it is obligatory to wear seat belts, otherwise, at best, you risk £25 to £60 fine.

  Children under 10 years of age must not sit at the front.

- First aid basic items, useful to have. The same applies to basic tools and spare parts.

- You may feel unhappy with some manners of driving if you are not used to it. The "priorite a droite" rule is exercised with a religious conviction, regardless of the situation, so do not try to apply logic of your own.If the unexpected takes place, just keep cool.

- If you break down always ask for an estimate before allowing repairs.

- Display the warning triangle in cases of emergency and, or have the hazard lights on.

- Free emergency telephones are sited at about 2km intervals along the autoroutes.Very often you will find them just in front of the Service Areas and most of them are marked in this guide. Once the emergency telephone is answered the Police will arrange road side assistance and medical service in case of an accident.

- Always check/compare your bill or credit card slip with the petrol pump indicator to agree both, before you pay or sign. Take the reading from the pump immediatly after delivery.

- Two grades of petrol are available: super — equivalent to 4-star, and normale (essence) — 2-star equivalent.

- At petrol stations additional services may be available if requested.

- On the Boulevard Peripherique keep in lane, at lea[st] second from the right hand side. The extreme right han[d] side lane driving can lead to some frustration as th[e] in-coming traffic joins the Boulevard in a manner as [if] there was nobody else driving. But the "Priorite a droite" rule, explains everything. Note ,that on roundabouts yo[u] may experience the same, although now, the traffic on th[e] roundabouts is governed by the same rules as in the UK[.] However, be watchful when approaching roundabout[s.] There are signed roundabouts bearing the words; "Vou[s] n'avez pas la priorite" (you do not have the right of wa[y) which simply means that the traffic on such roundabou[t] has priority. The other possible variation of the expressio[n] you may come across is; "Cedez le passage" - give wa[y.]

- Take special care if you decide to stop at the "zebr[a] crossing", because, if the road is wide enough, it is ver[y] likely that a local road user behind you will go past, thu[s] creating a dangerous situation.

- Note, that on the Continent the pedestrian has no "righ[t] of way" as in the UK.

- No doubt on many occasions you will become a pedestria[n] yourself. Watch out. As a pedestrian (who is used to th[e] "right of way" in the UK) you may occasionally want t[o] cross the road, and quite rightly opt for the "zebr[a] crossing". It cannot be overemphasised,that you loo[k] listen and wait for the right moment to cross the road an[d] be even more careful if a car stops in order to let you g[o] first. Especially important when accompanied by childre[n.]

- If you happen to drive through the town centre of Cala[is] on the way to Paris, you will face at a certain point a choic[e] to turn right for Paris and Boulogne, or left for St.Ome[r.] Take the route for St.Omer. Otherwise you will find yourse[lf] driving to Paris through Boulogne, along a secondary roa[d.]

- Always book your hotel and Channel crossing well i[n] advance, wherever possible.

- More formal appearance is required if you consider a vis[it] to some restaurants, theatres and casinos.

- On beaches, topless is a normal occurrence and is widel[y] accepted.

- As it is apparent from the conclusion of my researc[h] exercise in connection with this publication,that visitin[g] the South of France is a contagious "want", you may b[e] well advised therefore to start collecting a variety of goo[d] quality maps and relevant equipment which will prove t[o] be a good investment.

– Be aware of the fact that driving at a speed of 80 m p h you travel 40 yards in ONE second. Do not allow therefore, your concentration to lapse; take frequent breaks at Rest Areas.

– Do not ignore speed restrictions to the limits of stupidity which happens to be a common occurrence and very often the only explanation to the cause of many serious accidents.

– Always stop at level crossings to ensure safety, regardless of whether they are manned or not, or automatic.

– Beware of instances, where people approach you and ask for money for a variety of reasons. They would be well dressed, speak your language and tell you a story of how they were robbed or that their car has broken down, and they need your help (money).

– and now, be aware of a variety of salesmen who pretend at first to be lost or in need of some kind of help, and then they try to sell you goods. Do not allow yourself to be persuaded, under the pretext of seeing the goods, however attractive they may be, to enter the "salesman's" car.

– Watch out for drivers who do not indicate their intentions when on the road, especially when joining the traffic from a parking position.

– At some locations be aware of a plague of motoscooters and alike, buzzing from every angle of vision, and snaking along the road with apparent lack of concern for their own safety.

– Motoring laws are strictly enforced by the Police Road Patrol. The minimum fine for traffic offences, like ; speeding is around £130 or, for exceeding the drink-driving level, from £250 — £500, an equivalent of which in French currency is expected to be paid in cash on the spot. The members of the Patrol are very helpful otherwise, as well.

– According to the French Police records, about 50% of all accidents involving British cars takes place within 80 km of the Channel. In conclusion;do not rush rather opt for the next crossing.

Identity checks

The French Police can stop people in the streets, including foreigners, in order to check their identity, and in case of dissatisfaction with the outcome of the identification, a person can be taken to the police station for as long as it would be necessary to establish an identity.
(Another good reason to look after your documents)

MISCELLANEOUS

MINITEL SERVICE

This is an information service, provided by telephone-base
Minitel roadside computers which is available at some Res
Areas and often combined with "Bison Futé" enquiry desk
and central booking offices. This service will help you t
pinpoint traffic jams, indicate how much road tolls cost an
even help you find hotels and restaurants.

SPEED LIMITS — maximum, unless otherwise posted

	Road surface	
	Dry	Wet
Toll motorways	130 km/h	110 km/h
Dual carriageways and motorways without tolls	110 km/h	100 km/h
Other roads	90 km/h	80 km/h
In towns	60 km/h	60 km/h

In towns, the speed limit restriction begins with the "tow
name sign" and the restriction ends with the "town nam
sign" crossed diagonally.

Please note:

1. You must not exceed 90 km/h during the first year afte
passing your driving test.

2. There is a new minimum speed limit of 80 km/h (50 mph
for the outside lane on motorways, during daylight, on leve
ground and with good visibility.

BRITISH CONSULATES

Address in Paris;109 rue de Faubourg St-Honore,75008 –
Paris telephone;(1) 4266 — 9142.

There are also Consulates in the following towns; Bordeaux
Boulogne, Calais, Cherbourg, Dunkirk, Le Havre, Lille, Lyor
Marseille, Nantes and Perpignan.

— And finally, the French road network is clasified by;
   A — Motorway (Autorote),
   N — National roads,
   D — Regional roads (Departamentale),
   V — Local roads (Chemins vicinaux).

FRENCH NATIONAL HOLIDAYS

(Jour Férié)

January 1	*Jour de L'An*	New Year's Day
May 1	*Fête du Travail*	Labour Day
May 8	VE Day	
July 14	*Fête Nationale*	Bastille Day
August 15	*Assumption*	Assumption
November 1	*Toussaint*	All Saints
November 11	*Anniversaire de L'Armistice*	Armistice Day
December 25	*Noel*	Christmas

Moveable dates

Lundi de Pâques	Easter Monday
Ascension	Ascension
Lundi de Pentecôte	Whit Monday

The week-ends incorporating July 14 and August 15, are the ideal dates to break your journey and stay in Paris. On the motorway and everywhere else will be very heavy traffic. Except Paris, hotels along the motorway are very likely to be fully booked, well in advance.

CORRELATIVE VOCABULARY

Days of the Week

Monday	*lundi*
Tuesday	*mardi*
Wednesday	*mercredi*
Thursday	*jeudi*
Friday	*vendredi*
Saturday	*samedi*
Sunday	*dimanche*

Months of the Year

January	*janvier*
February	*fevrier*
March	*mars*
April	*avril*
May	*mai*
June	*juin*
July	*juillet*
August	*août*
September	*septembre*
October	*octobre*
November	*novembre*
December	*decembre*

Numbers

1 — un (une)		21 — vingt et un
2 — deux		22 — vingt deux
3 — trois		23 — vingt trois etc.,
4 — quatre		30 — trente
5 — cinq		31 — trente et un
6 — six		32 — trente deux
7 — sept		33 — trente troix
8 — huit		40 — quarante
9 — neuf		50 — cinquante
10 — dix		60 — sixante
11 — onze		70 — soixante-dix
12 — douze		80 — quatre-vingt
13 — treize		90 — quatre-vingt-dix
14 — quatorze		100 — cent
15 — quinzè		101 — cent-un
16 — seize		102 — cent deux
17 — dix-sept		200 — deux cents
18 — dix-huit		500 — cinq cents
19 — dix-neuf		1000 — mille
20 — vingt		2000 — deux mille

How to book your room in a hotel

Je voudrais reserver... *I would like to book...*
Une chambre avec ... *one room with...*

— un lit — *one bed, or*
— deux lits — *two beds, or*
— grand lit — *double bed*
— douche — *shower*
— salle de bain — *bathroom*
— pour ce soir — *for this evening*
— pour trois jours — *for three days*

Le petit dejeuner — *breakfast*
Le prix par jour — *rate per night*
La pension complète — *full board*
La demi-pension — *half board (bed and breakfast and evening meal)*
Une emplacement pour une voiture — *space for one car*

Some more expressions, but now from English to French:

Good morning — *bonjour*
Good afternoon — *bonjour*
Good evening — *bonsoir*
Good bye — *au revoir*

please — *s'il vous plait*
how are you — *comment allez-vous*
very well, thank you — *tres bien, merci.*
it is a nice day — *il fait beau*
it is hot — *il fait chaud*
it is cold — *il fait froid*
I do not speak French — *je ne parle pas français*
I do not know — *je ne sais pas*
here is the key — *voici le clef*
to do the shopping — *faire des courses*
good luck — *bon courage, bonne chance*
underground — *metro*
careful, look out — *attention*
to your health, cheers — *à votre santé*
accommodation — *logement*
Money — *l'argent*
excuse me — *excusez-moi*
yesterday — *hier*
today — *aujourd'hui*
Midday — *midi*
tomorrow — *demain*
change — *monnaie (more meaning of coins)*
footbridge — *la passerelle*
push — *poussez*
pull — *tirez*

Some parts of the car and associated vocabulary:

Battery — *Batterie*
Flat battery — *Batterie à vide)*
Bonnet — *Capot*
Car — *Voiture*
Carburettor — *Carburateur*
Distributor — *Distributeur d'allumage*
Points — *Jeu de contacts)*
Door — *Porte*   Car door – *Portière*
Fan belt — *Courroie*
Fuse box — *Boite à fusibles*
Gasket (seal) — *Joint*
Gearbox - *Boite de vitesse*
Grease — *Lubricant*
Headlamp — *Phare*
Horn — *Avertisseur*
Hose — *Durite*
Ignition system — *Systèm d'allumage*
Number Plate – *Plaque de police*

Oil — *Huile*
Oil level — *Niveau d'huile*
Oil change — *Vidange*
Oil leak — *Fuite d'huile*
Petrol tank — *Reservoir d'essence*
Puncture — *Crevaison*
Radiator — *Radiateur*
Seat belt — *Ceinture de sécurité*
Side lamp — *Feu de position*
Spark plug — *Bougie*
Tyre — *Pneu*
Water — *Eau*
Wheel — *Roue*
Windscreen — *Pare-brise*

My car is broken down — *ma voiture est en panne*
Something is wrong with .... — *Quelque chose ne va pa*

the engine — *dans le moteur*
the brakes — *aux freins*

Car logbook — *carte grise*
Driving licence — *permis de conduire*
4-star petrol — *essence super (Super)*
2-star petrol — *essence normale (Essence)*
Unleaded petrol – *Sans plomb*

CONVERSION TABLES AND FACTORS

Length

1 inch (in) =	25.4 millimetres (mm)
=	2.54 centimetres (cm)
1 foot (ft) =	30.48 (cm)
=	0.3048 metre (m)
1 yard (yd) =	91.44 (cm)
=	0.9144 (m)
1 mile =	1.609 kilometres (km)
1 centimetre (cm) =	0.394 inch (in)
1 metre (m) =	1.094 yards (yd)
1 kilometre (km) =	0.621 mile

olume

$$1 \text{ UK ounce} = 28.41 \text{ cm}$$
$$= 28.41 \text{ millilitres (ml)}$$
$$1 \text{ pint (pt)} = 0.568 \text{ litre (l)}$$
$$1 \text{ UK gallon (UK gal)} = 4.546 \text{ litres}$$
$$1 \text{ litre (l)} = 0.22 \text{ UK gallon}$$
$$= 1.76 \text{ pint}$$

Weight

$$1 \text{ pound (lb)} = 0.454 \text{ kilogram (kg)}$$
$$1 \text{ hundredweight (cwt)} = 50.8 \text{ kilograms (kg)}$$
$$1 \text{ UK ton} = 1016.05 \text{ kg}$$
$$= 1.016 \text{ metric tonnes}$$

$$1000 \text{ kg} = 1 \text{ metric tonne (t)}$$
$$1 \text{ kg} = 2.2 \text{ pounds (lb)}$$
$$1 \text{ metric tonne (t)} = 2204.62 \text{ (lb)}$$
$$= 0.984 \text{ UK ton}$$

ressure

$$1 \text{ pound per square inch}$$
$$(\text{lb/in}) = .069 \text{ kg/cm}$$
$$1 \text{ kg/cm} = 14.2 \text{ (ib/in)}$$

yre pressure

b/in)	(kg/cm)	(ib/in)	(kg/cm)
1	0.07	32	2.25
5	0.35	33	2.32
10	0.70	34	2.39
15	1.05	35	2.46
16	1.12	36	2.53
17	1.20	37	2.60
18	1.27	38	2.67
19	1.34	39	2.74
20	1.41	40	2.81
21	1.48	41	2.88
22	1.55	42	2.95
23	1.62	43	3.02
24	1.69	44	3.09
25	1.76	45	3.16
26	1.83	46	3.23
27	1.90	47	3.30
28	1.97	48	3.37
29	2.04	49	3.45
30	2.11	50	3.52
31	2.18	51	3.59

Temperature

Conversion of degrees Centigrade into Fahrenheit

C	0	5	10	15	20	25	30	35	
F	32	41	50	59	68	77	86	95	1(

Fuel consumption

Conversion of (miles/gallon) into (litres/100 kilometres)

miles/gallon	litres/100 km
10	28.25
15	18.84
20	14.13
25	11.30
30	9.42
35	8.07
40	7.06
45	6.28
50	5.65

1 (mile per gallon) = 282.54 (litre/100 km)

A VOUS PARIS

ıy a courtesy of the French Government Tourist Office in ındon)

ıe tall houses of Paris, the tree — lined boulevards, the stone ıidges and precisely laid-out parks are as lovely on a snowy ıinter's day as in the summer sunshine, as enchanting in the ıle light of dawn as in the twinkle street lights at dusk. It ı an unfailingly beguiling city, and of the world's capital, ırhaps the most agreeable to visit.

ıot only enchanting to look at, it offers endless pleasures to ıss the hours; beautiful paintings... haunting views... smart ırs...ancient cafes drenched in atmosphere... opera... ırkish baths...museums...gardens...restaurants that perfect ıery conceivable type of cooking. Countless book and ıides eulogise the marvels of Paris, and they enhance any ıp.

ıe City is divided into 20 districts or *arrondissements*, ımbered,very conveniently, from one to twenty.The ımbering starts in the heart of Paris, then spirals, putting ıe twentieth district - the *vingtième* - in the far east. ıestaurants, bars, hotels and museums are all listed in guides ıccording to their district, and it makes more sense of a map ı you know roughly where each district lies.

ıe first includes the Louvre, the Palais-Royal, the Tuileries ıardens, the place Vendôme, the Ritz and the Comédie ıancaise the elegant Rue de Rivoli, and plenty of hotels; then ıosses the river Seine to encompass Sainte - Chapelle and ıalf of the Ile de la Cité.

ıe *deuxième* runs north of the first and includes the Opéra ıea, where many of the city's most prestigious hotels and ıeatres are located and, in the east, a number of less ıxpensive hotels.

ıe *troisième* is old Paris; the Marais, once the smartest area ı Paris and now smartly restored after centuries of neglect. ıhere are few hotels here but plenty in the fourth district, ıhich takes in part of the Marais, the new Centre ıompidou,the other half of the Ile de la Cité, and the whole ı the Ile St-Louis.

These four *arrondissements* are all on the right bank —
north of the river Seine. Getting to the fifth or cinquièn
means a hop across the river into the Latin Quarter. Here
the Sorbonne University, the busy Boulevard St-Michel wi
all the cafes, the Jeu de Paume gallery and, in the sixth, sma
nightclubs.

Eiffel tower is situated squarely in the *septième*, along wi
Les Invalides, Napoleon's great tomb, a number
government buildings, and residential streets.

The eight district is fashionable, expensive and rather wi
homes of luxurious hotels, the Champs - Elysées, the Lid
and the Crazy Horse cabaret club, as well as the huge Pla
de la Concorde, the presidential palace, and the ve
fashionable Rue du Faubourg St-Honoré.

The ninth containes plenty of contrast: department store
theatres, the Opera, and blowsy Pigalle. In the tenth only tl
Gare du Nord and the Gare de L'Est occupy visitors muc
and in the residential eleventh, twelfth and thirteenth distric
there is little of interest to outsiders.

The fourteenth has the huge Tour Montparnasse and a lar
Sheraton hotel; the fifteenth, mysterious little streets, full
interesting shops, and some modern luxury hotels; tl
sixteenth, smart Avenue Foch the Bois de Boulogne, and li
the seventeenth, comfortable, old — fashioned hotels.

The eighteenth is dominated by Montmartre, and the lof
Sacre — Coeur, while the nineteenth and *vingtième* a
mainly residential areas. And when you run out of numbe
you have the green and wooded country of the Ile — de
France which cradles Paris. Its Royal lands harbour châtea
and manor houses, cathedrals and churches, chapels ar
abbeys — and over a hundred museums.

NEW PARIS

PLUS ÇA CHANGE PLUS C'EST LA M E ME CHOSE is
useful piece of French wisdom that applies to almc
everything, except perhaps the French capital. Anyone doii
the rounds there recently will have been aware of striking ne
silhouettes taking shape on the skyline and an element
surprise in some public spaces.

The intestinal tract of the Pompidou Art Centre, once dubbed the oil refinery" has, by sheer dint of having been there several years, wormed its way into the affections of Parisians and tourists alike — just as the city's beloved trademark, the Eiffel Tower, rose above the insults hurled at its erection in the 19th century — "a great black factory chimney" they called it before the paint had time to dry.

PLUS ÇA CHANGE...

Pompidou is now an unmissable sight, both outside and in, for its exciting exhibitions, collections of 20th century art, and its looks which have proved that a building has a role as entertainer. Visitors are so amused by the escalators as they're processed through exterior glass tubes that, like befuddled actors, they miss their exits and entrances.

Nearby, the now virtually completed Forum shopping complex is a far cry from the blot on the landscape it was feared might accumulate here when the old Les Halles market area was ripped up. Since the various levels burrow downwards, the lovely old church of St -Eustache is clearly visible and the bonestructure of the Forum's conservatorial corridors echoes the lines of the Gothic church's flying buttresses. The Forum is also an enjoyable place to be: a shopper's club — sandwich of designer boutiques and BON MARCH E, CROISSANTERIES and other fast food dispensaries, emporia selling just-about- anything-you-can-think-of. And for those who still hanker after onion soup in the small hours, there are plenty of restaurants in the surrounding web of streets that still serve the brown, cheese-topped broth in varying strengths.

Latest addition to this area is the pool and fountains betwixt the Pompidou Centre and the shadowy church of St-Merri — an incongruous but delightful water gallery for the work of two sculptors: Tinguely,whose whimsical Heath — Robinsonesque clockworks twirl in the centre, and Nicky de St-Phalle, whose brightly coloured fibre-glass sculptures never fail to raise a smile, an eyebrow or the temperature of passers-by. Luscious lips and a nubile torso fairly whack you between the eyes. They certainly lift the atmosphere of this once — faded little square where now new pavement cafes are spreading across the cobbles.

So brave and new it's not yet finished, is the vast science industry and culture complex at La Villette on the north- east outskirts of Paris. Here, some of the most visually stunning architecture of the Eighties wraps up this city-within-a-city designed for learning and leisure. Focal point is the Geode, a spectacular 117ft — wide spherical cinema, created by Fainsilber. Outside, its mirror-finish conjures fantastic moving pictures from the reflections of its surroundings.

The huge Centre of Science and Industry, opposite, summon
every audio — visual and computerised aid to present th
acceptable — and understandable — face of technolog
Then there's the Grande Halle, a former cattle mark
revamped by architects Reichen and Robert as a venue fc
shows and exhibitions.

La Villette already has theatres and creative workshop
concert halls and conference centres, a bumper park an
gardens where children can explore, discover and play. Mor
is being added year by year — a City of Music next. You hav
to bear this in mind when you visit, for uncultivated parts sti
resound to a cacophony of construction. But this needn
worry you as the whole thing is so huge and there's so muc
to see you can easily stay clear of the bulldozers. How to ge
there? Metro Porte La Villette or take your car- there's
mammoth underground car park.

TRANSPORT IN PARIS   (Métro, Bus, RER, RATP

(Ed.Information supplied by the FGTO)

WHERE DO YOU BUY YOUR TICKET ?

Most categories of ticket can be bought; in all Métro or REF
(Le Réseau Express Réginal - Métro Régional) stations, in a
ticket offices at bus terminals, in some tobacconists.

"Carte orange" and "Formule 1" tickets are also on sale i
SNCF Railway stations within the Paris area.

"Seasame tickets" (tourist tickets) can be bought in mai
metro & RER stations, in SNCF (La Société Nationale de
Chemins de Fer Français) Railway stations in Paris an
airports (Charles de Gaulle & Orly), in RATP (Régie Autor
ome des Transports Parisiens) sales office situated: 53 bi
Quai des Grands Augustins, 75006 - Paris, or Place de I
Madeleine, 75008 - Paris, and also in some hotels, banks
travel agencies.

In the U.K., tourist tickets can be bought from "Continenta
shipping", 179 Piccadilly, London, W1V 9DB
RATP Information: Tel. (1) 4346-1414

ATEGORIES OF TICKET AVAILABLE

. - For one journey or more; single tickets.

ou can buy one single ticket or a book of 10 tickets.

On the métro: one single ticket is valid for one journey, whatever the distance of the journey, with or without changes.

On bus routes, each route is divided into sections. One ticket is valid for one or 2 sections. For 3 sections or more 2 tickets are needed within the central Paris area (Bus routes numbered less than 100) and from 2 to 6 tickets are needed for buses outside Paris (Bus routes numbered over 100) and for circular Bus: "P.C".

On the RER tariff varies according to length of journey, except for the following RER lines within Paris:

- line A between "Etoile" & "Nation"
- line B between "Gare du Nord" & "Gentilly"
- line C between "Boulevard Victor" & "Boulevard Mas-séna"
- line D between "Gare du Nord' & "Châtelet-les-Halles"

here the same tariff as the métro applies, irrespective of ngth of journey, allowing changes from metro lines to RER

eyond this central section price of tickets varies according to ngth of journey.

ickets	2nd class	1st class
ticket (bus or metro)	5.00 F	7.20 F
arnet of 10 tickets		
full price	30.00 F	46.00 F
reduced price	15.00 F	23.00 F
ER tickets from Paris		
outskirts.	up to	up to
full price	16.00 F	24.60 F
reduced price	8.00 F	12.30 F

educed (half - price) tickets are available for the following ategories :

children from 4 to 10 years (children under 4 travel free),

groups of at least 10 young people under 16 years ccompanied by an adult.

Requests for these ("demandes de transport") must be made on a printed form available from all metro stations and must be presented at the beginning of the journey. The group leader is also entitled to the reduction (1 leader for each group of ten people).

Please note, this reduction does not apply on buses.

B - "Season" Tickets for Unlimited Travel.

All the season tickets described below allow unlimited travel within a zone, on métro, bus and RER, and in some cases on SNCF suburban networks and on APTR (Private buses under contract to the RATP) bus lines. They are not transferable.

There are five zones numbered from 1 to 5 : zone 1 covers Paris, zones 2 to 5 cover concentric zones around the capital.

* For 1 Day: "FORMULE 1" Ticket.

"Formule 1" includes an identity card (Without photograph) and a ticket (coupon) valid for one day. It can be bought in advance and is valid on RATP and SNCF networks, métro, bus, RER, commuter trains to Paris outskirts and Montmartre cable railway.

Formule 1	2nd Class
Zones 1 - 2	20.00
Zones 1 - 2 - 3	24.00
Zones 1 - 2 - 3 - 4 (*)	35.00
Formule 1 Airports zones	
1 - 2 - 3 - 4 + Orly-bus, Orly-rail	
and Roissy - rail	60.00

(*) – Not valid on Orly-bus and Orly-rail

* For 2, 4 or 7 days: "PARIS SESAME" Card (Tourist Ticket).

"Paris - sesame" is valid for either 2,4, or 7 consecutive days. It entitles you to unlimited travel on all RATP network (on SNCF network different tariffs will apply), metro lines and R.E.R. (A & B south of "Gare du Nord") in 1st Class carriages, buses (except special bus routes) and on Montmartre cable railway.

Please note: it is not valid on the SNCF network, nor APTR lines.

On metro lines and RER insert the magnetic card attached to the ticket in the slot of the electronic gate (except on the RER line B south of "Les Baconnets"). On regular bus routes, the ticket must be shown to the driver.

aris - Sesame

	1st Class
days	57.00 F
days	85.00 F
days	141.00 F

For one week or one month; "Carte Orange".

ou need one photocard.
one yellow ticket (coupon jaune): for one week, valid from
onday to Sunday (inclusive, on sale until Wednesday)
one orange ticket (coupon orange): for one month, valid
om 1st to last day of the month, and on sale from the 20th of
e preceding month.
iese can be used; on all metro lines, buses, RER, SNCF
uburban trains, APTR buses, and Montmartre cable railway.

arte Orange

	Weekly (yellow ticket)		Monthly (orange ticket)	
	2nd Class	1st Class	2nd Class	1st Class
one 1 - 2	49.00 F	73.00 F	170.00 F	255.00 F
one 1 - 2 & 3	63.00 F	101.00 F	219.00 F	353.00 F
one 1 - 2 & 3 - 4	86.00 F	147.00 F	300.00 F	515.00 F
one 1 - 5	104.00 F	183.00 F	362.00 F	639.00 F

For 2 daily journeys within a week; "Carte Hebdoma-
ire".

ie "Carte hebdomadaire 12 voyages" (12 Journeys) allows
daily journeys over 6 days, within a period of 7 consecutive
ays. It is not transferable.

arte Hebdomadaire

	2nd Class
etro - RER within Paris centre	28.50 F
ER Paris and outskirts	up to 80.00 F
us 1 - 2 "sections"	26.00 F
us 3 - 5 "sections"	46.00 F (*)
us 6 "sections" and over	from 65 F to 84 F

maximum price for central Paris bus lines, lines numbered
der 100.

Cinema seats

First release	33.00 FF	to	39.00 F
(students, Senior Citizens, and Mondays)	20.00	to	29.00

Entrance prices for cabarets

Folies Bergere	82.00 FF	to	350.00 F
The Lido (Champagne and Show)			350.00
Dinner and Show			510.00
The Moulin Rouge, Champagne and Show			350.00
Dinner and Show			510.00
To Crazy Horse Show + 2 drinks			460.00
The Paradis Latin Champagne and Show			350.00
Dinner and Show			510.00
The Bateaux Mouches Dinner and cruise			450.00

Museums and historic monuments

Entrance fees for National museum vary between 10 and 20 FF.
The Louvre: 20 FF, free on Sundays. All National Museum offer 50 % reductions on Sundays and Public Holidays.

Conciergerie - Sainte - Chapelle	22.00 F
Arc de Triomphe, by stairs	9.00
Eiffel Tower : 2nd floor, by stairs	7.00
by lift	28.00
3rd floor, by lift	44.00
Tour Montparnasse (59 floor)	31.00
children	18.50
Notre - Dame: the church	free
the towers	15.00

Reduced rates of admission for children, students and seni citizens are available.

There are numerous tourist companies which offer sigl seeing tours, lasting for a duration of a few hours to a full da featuring, tightly scheduled excursions; to see Paris by d and, to see Paris by night.

The hotels of Paris shown in the Guide will be able to advi you in detail, on how to tackle the town of Paris, efficiently, all aspects of its attractions. Some of the hotels (e.g.ARCAL - Cambronne) houses a Tourist Information Service De which may arrange everything for you.

FOLIES BERGÈRE

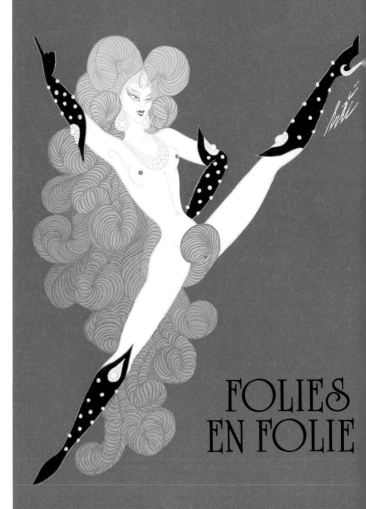

FOLIES EN FOLIE

GALERIES Lafayette

The department store capital of fashion.

GALERIES LAFAYETTE
welcomes Touring Motorists

*Welcome service with english speaking hostesses
*Parking garage with 1,000 car capacity
*A world overflowing with gift and souvenir ideas

40, bd Haussmann, 75009 Paris 9:30-18:30 Mon.-Sat.

HOTELS IN PARIS

★ ★ ★ ★ de Luxe	Telephone	Page
A Pullman St.Jacques	4589-8980	70

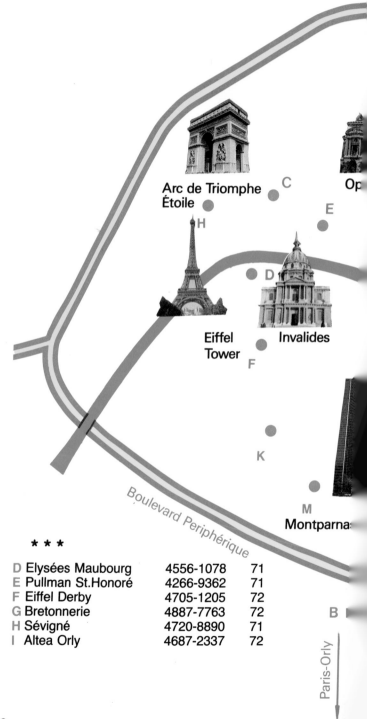

Arc de Triomphe
Étoile

C

Op

E

H

D

Eiffel Tower

F

Invalides

K

M

Montparna

Boulevard Periphérique

★ ★ ★

D Elysées Maubourg	4556-1078	71
E Pullman St.Honoré	4266-9362	71
F Eiffel Derby	4705-1205	72
G Bretonnerie	4887-7763	72
H Sévigné	4720-8890	71
I Altea Orly	4687-2337	72

B

Paris-Orly

★ ★ ★ ★

B	Pullman Paris-Orly	4687-3636	70
C	Pullman Windsor	4563-0404	70

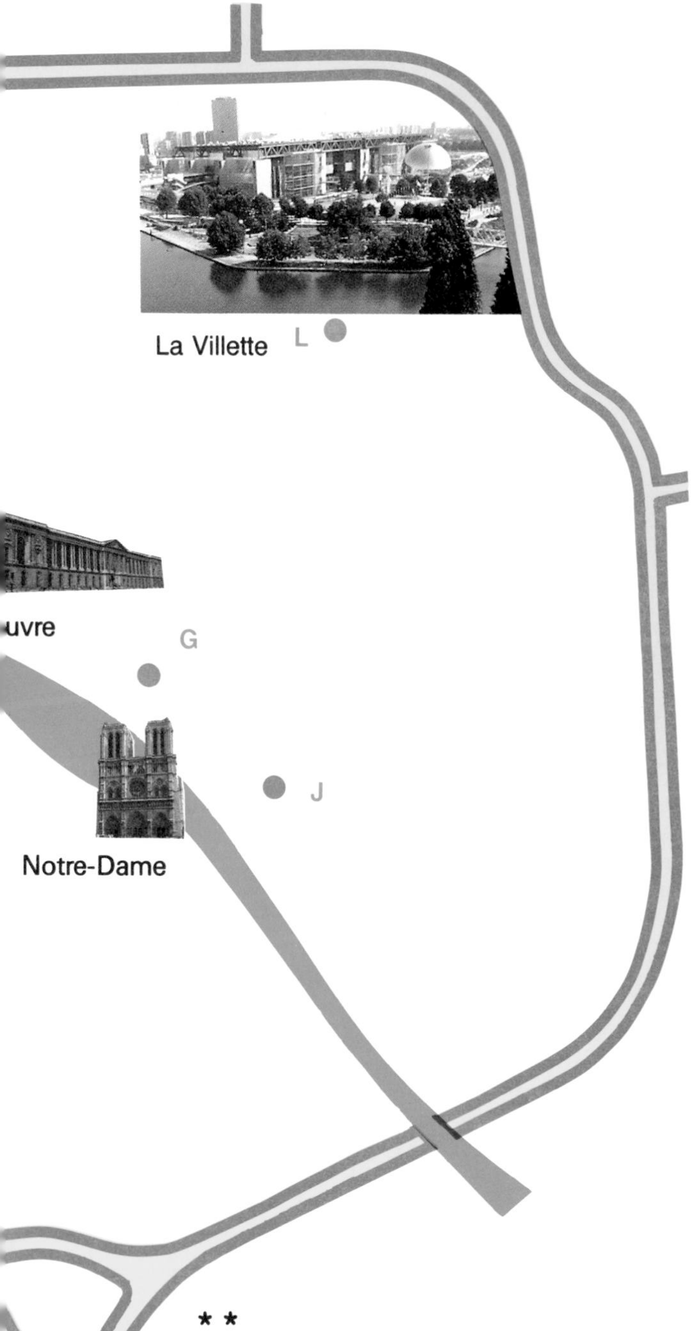

La Villette L ●

uvre

G ●

J ●

Notre-Dame

★ ★

J	Arcade-Bastille	4268-2345	74
K	Arcade-Cambronne	4567-3520	74
L	Arcade-La Villette	4038-0404	73
M	Arcade-Montparnasse	4567-3520	74

PULLMAN SAINT-JACQUES **** de Luxe

17 Boulevard Saint-Jacques,
75014 — Paris
Tel.(1) 4589-8980, Telex: 270740

 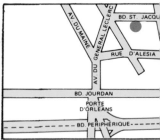

800 rooms ● bathrooms ● air-conditioning ● radio ● colo
TV ● mini-bar ● direct line telephone ● 5 restaurants — japanes
chinese and famous "Cafe Francais" ● 2 bars ● 17 conferen
rooms ● travel agency car rental ● cinema ● shoppi
arcade ● beauty salon ● garage ● bus to airport

PULLMAN PARIS-ORLY ****

20 Avenue C.Lindbergh
94656 — Rungis Cedex
Tel.(1) 4687-3636, Telex:260 738

206 rooms ● details, page 14 ● room service ● TV with video circuit
restaurant ● parking facilities ● hotel shuttle bus free ● garden ● b
● boutique ● sauna bath ● open-air swiming pool ● close to Rung
wholesale market ● 20 min drive from Paris and near the Orly airpor

PULLMAN WINDSOR ****

14, Rue Beaujon,
75008 — Paris
Tel.(1) 4563-0404, Telex: 650 — 902

 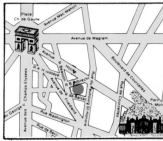

135 rooms ● details page 14 ● TV with video circuit ● restaurant ● ba
● meeting rooms.

HOTEL ELYSÉES-MAUBOURG ★★★

35 Boulevard de Latour Maubourg,
75007 Paris
Tel.(1) 4556-1078, Telex:206 227 F

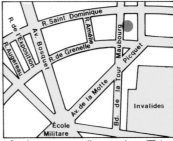

rooms with fully equipped private bathroom ● radio ● colour TV ●
ni-bar ● personal safe box in each room ● direct telephone ● sauna
small garden ● bar ● rooms with video in English and cable TV- at
ur disposal; cable TV (channel 4) and video film (channel 8). A new
n each night at 9 p.m. and 11 p.m.

PULLMAN ST.HONORE ★★★

15 Rue Boissy — d'Anglas,
75008 — Paris
Tel.(1) 4266-9362, Telex: 240366

2 rooms ● duplexes and suite ● bathroom ● radio ● colour TV with
deo circuit with in house movie channel ● mini-bar ● direct
lephone ● bar ● parking nearby.

HOTEL DE SÉVIGNÉ ★★★

6 Rue de Belloy,
75116 — Paris
Tel.(1) 4720-8890, Telex:610219 F

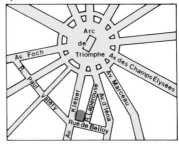

0 rooms with bathrooms ● colour TV ● radio ● direct telephone ●
nini-bar ● bar ● laundry and dry cleaning ● safe ● car rental ●
arking facilities.

DERBY EIFFEL HOTEL ***

5 Avenue Duquesne,
75007 — Paris
Tel.(1) 4705-1205, Telex:Derby 206236

 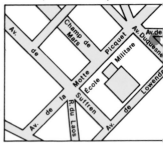

44 rooms with private bathrooms, WC ● colour TV ● direct telephon
● sound-proofed ● personal safety deposit box in each room ● priva
bar ● small garden.

HOTEL DE LA BRETONNERIE ***

22 Rue Ste Croix de la Bretonnerie,
75004 — Paris
Tel.(1) 4887-7763

31 rooms with fully equipped bathrooms ● this unique hote
recommended in a 17th century mansion house will make you fe
a real inhabitant of Old Paris ● direct-line telephone ● period furnitur

ALTEA HOTEL ***

429-94547 Orly Aerogare Cedex,
Tel.(1) 4687-2337, Telex:204 345

 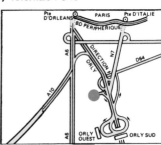

200 rooms with fully equipped bathrooms ● sound proofed ● TV wit
video ciccuit ● air-conditioned ● radio ● restaurant ● bar ● parking
free shuttle service to the airport ● 800 m from Orly air terminals
close to the International Rungis market.

HOTEL ARCADE-PARIS LA VILLETTE **

31-35 Quai de L'Oise
75019 – Paris
Tel.4038-0404, Telex: Arcvilt 218731

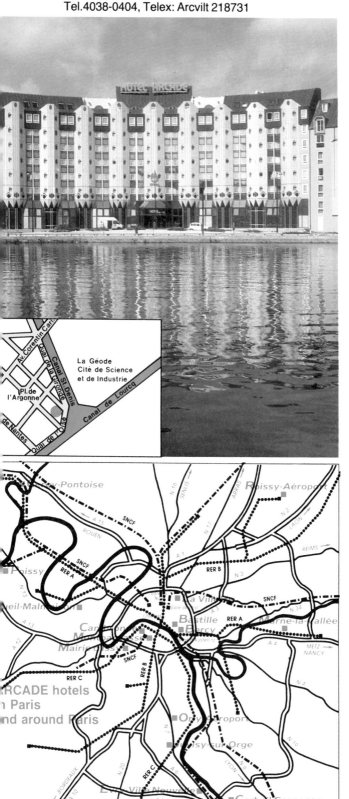

HOTEL ARCADE PARIS ★★

2 Rue de Cambronne,
75740 — Paris, Cedex 15
Tel. (1) 4567-3520, Telex: Arcapar 203842

530 rooms

TYPICAL EXAMPLE OF THE ARCADE HOTELS

All rooms with shower and WC ● telephone ● alarm clock ● colour
on request ● restaurant ● bar ● nursery ● tourist and entertainme
information ● boutique – duty free ● parking facilities.

HOTEL ARCADE PARIS-BASTILLE ★★

Angle rue bréguet/rue Frome
75011 – Paris
Tel. 4567-3520, Telex: 2038

310 rooms

HOTEL ARCADE
PARIS-MONTPARNASSE ★★

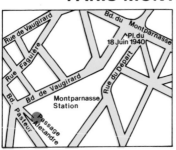

15 Passage Alexandre
75015 — Paris

31 rooms

ARCADE HOTELS IN FRANCE

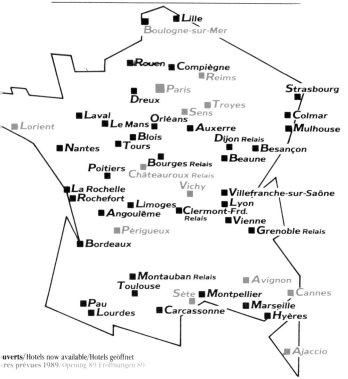

JXERRE, Avenue Jean-Jaurés, Tel.8648-1055

VIGNON, 12 Bd.St.Dominique/Pont de l'Europe, el.(1)4268-2345 (Opens June 89)

EAUNE, Avenue du Gal. de Gaulle/Rond Point de l'Europe, el.8022-7567

LOIS, Espace St.Vincent, 4 rue Jean Moulin, Tel.5478-2414

ORDEAUX St.Jean, 60 rue Eugène Le Roy, Tel.5691-4040

OULOGNE S/Mer, Angle Bd. Eurvin/rue Porte Neuve, el.(1)4268-2345

ARCASSONNE, 5 Square Gambetta, Tel.6872-3737

OMPIEGNE, 10 rue Pierre Sauvage, Tel.4486-0066

JON, 15 bis Avenue Albert 1er, Tel.8043-0112

YERES, 14 Avenue de la 1er Div.Brosset, Tel.9465-4748

LLE, 172 rue de Paris, 2030-0054

YON La Part Dieu, 78 rue de Bonnel, Tel.7862-9889

ARSEILLE, Square Narvick-Gare SNCF St.Charles, el.9195-6209

ONTPELLIER, Bd. d'Antigone, Tel.6764-0664

RLEANS, 4 rue du Mal. Foch, Tel.3854-2311

OITIERS, Angle du Petit Bonneveau/rue Carnot, Tel.4988-042

OUEN St.Sever, Place de L'Eglise St.Sever-River Gauche, el.3562-8182

ETE, 60 Quai de Bosc, Tel.(1)4268-2345 (Opens April 89)

OULOUSE, 2 rue Claire Pauilhac (Place Jeanne d'Arc), el.6163-6163

OURS, 1 rue GeorgeClaude (angle rue Edouard Vailland), el.4761-4444

IENNE, Place Camille Jouffray, Tel.7485-4646

ILLEFRANCHE S/SAONE, 146 rue de la Sous-Préfecture, el.7462-0104

DISCOVER la Villette

La Villette : a new way of seeing, listening, learning, (amazement and emotion ! A place for creativity an(leisure, for discovery and play.**

The Cité des Sciences et de l'Industrie at La Villett(Parc : You'll be surprised how much fun learning can be Here's what the Cité has to offer :
- Interactive areas where visitors can get involved
- Shows at the Planetarium, the Cine-Club and **the Géo(de** (on a 11,000 square-foot screen)
- Fascinating exhibitions, activities for children (3 year(and up)

A huge multimedia library, shops and unusual gifts mu(tilingual information staff.

La Villette is above all a park of thirty five hectare((eighty seven acres), the largest in Paris. A lively exciting place to play, familiarize oneself with com(puters, learn about gardening or attend concerts...

The Grande Halle – a space for all events with its mov(able, transformable equipment, the Great Hall adapt(itself to the needs of cultural as well as technical o(scientific performances.

The Zenith – a concert hall specifically created for po(and rock music. It can hold up to 6,400 people.

The Paris-Villette Theater

In 1989, **the City of Music :** an array of equipmer(indispensable for the teaching of music and the pro(fessional training of musicians.

**Cité des Sciences
et de l'Industrie**
Architect :
Adrien Fainsilber
Photo : J.Y. Gregoire

The Grande Halle
Architect :
Reichen and Robert
Photo : Ph. Gras

One of the park "Folies"
Architect :
Bernard Tschumi
Photo : J.M. Monthiers

Bamboo garden
Architect :
Alexandre Chemetoff
Photo : J.M. Monthiers

Addresses :

• **Park, Grande Halle, Zenith,
Paris-Villette Theater,
City of Music :
211, avenue Jean-Jaurès
75019 Paris
Answering machine
42 78 70 00**

• **Cité des Sciences
et de l'Industrie, Geode
30, avenue Corentin Cariou
75019 Paris
Answering machine
40 05 72 72**

GALERIES Lafayette

The Department Store Capital of Fashion, established in 1895.

The famous dome, shown above, is 100 feet in diameter which due to its originality, has become an admired attraction for tourists visiting the Department Store in which the efficient service, provided by the highly qualified multilingual staff, guides you smoothly through all the stages of your shopping.

Galeries Lafayette has become an important place where all the greatest names and designers meet with their latest achievements.

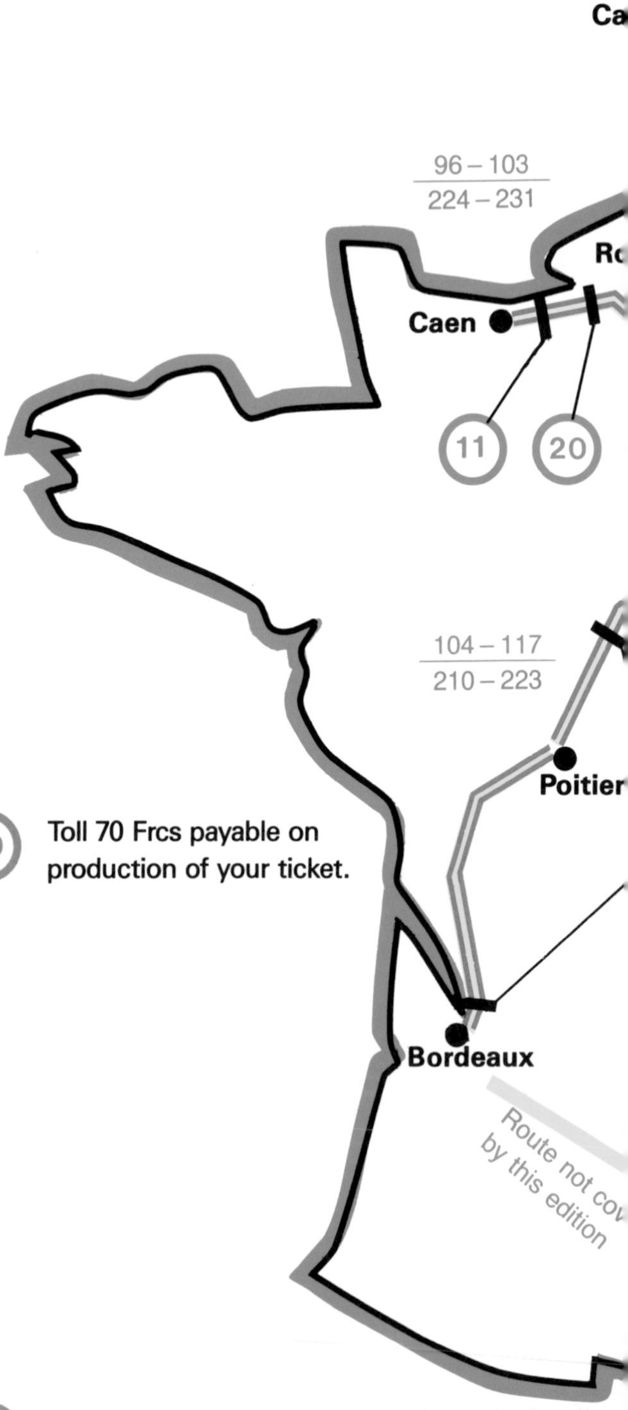

Ca

$$\frac{96 - 103}{224 - 231}$$

Rc

Caen ●

11   20

$$\frac{104 - 117}{210 - 223}$$

Poitier

70 Toll 70 Frcs payable on
production of your ticket.

Bordeaux

Route not cov
by this edition

7 Toll 7 Frcs payable at the automatic service barrière
péage, have your coins ready. Use separate, mark
lane if change is required.

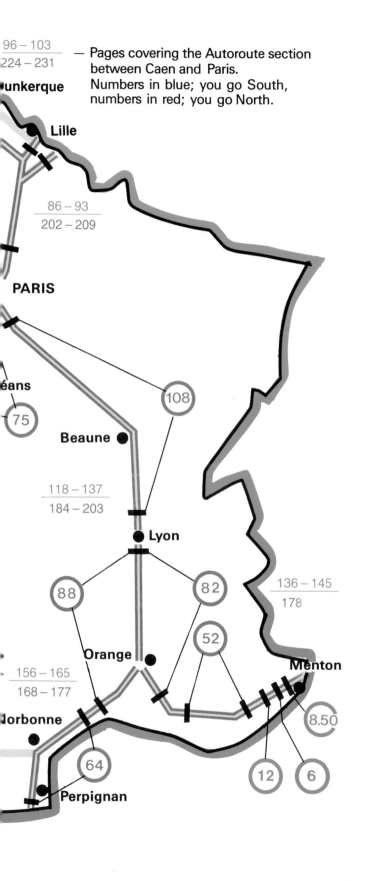

96 – 103
224 – 231

— Pages covering the Autoroute section
between Caen and Paris.
Numbers in blue; you go South,
numbers in red; you go North.

unkerque

Lille

86 – 93
202 – 209

PARIS

éans

75

108

Beaune

118 – 137
184 – 203

Lyon

88

82

136 – 145
178

52

Orange

Menton

156 – 165
168 – 177

lorbonne

8.50

64

12

6

Perpignan

L'ARCHE RESTAURANTS

RESTAURANT FORMULAS - LEGEND

A - BAR - SANDWICHERIE
B - SELF-SERVICE
C - GRILL - SERVICE AT TABLE

Nearest town

ON MOTORWAY A.1

L'ARCHE	de	RESSONS-Est	A-B	COMPIEGNE
L'ARCHE	de	RESSONS-Ouest	B	COMPIEGNE
L'ARCHE	d'	ASSEVILLERS-Est	B	PERONNE
L'ARCHE	d'	ASSEVILLERS-Ouest	A-B-C	PERONNE

ON MOTORWAY A.31

L'ARCHE	de	SANDAUCOURT	B	VITTEL

ON MOTORWAY A.4

L'ARCHE	de	VERDUN	A-B-C	VERDUN

ON MOTORWAY A.6

L'ARCHE	de	VENOY-Ouest	A-B	AUXERRE
L'ARCHE	de	VENOY-Est	B-C	AUXERRE
L'ARCHE	de	MAISON DIEU	B	AVALLON
L'ARCHE	de	SAINT-AMBREUIL	B	CHALON S/S
L'ARCHE	de	SAINT-ALBAIN	A-B-C	MACON

ON MOTORWAY A.9

L'ARCHE	de	FABREGUES	A-B-C	MONTPELLIER

ON MOTORWAY A.7				
L'ARCHE	de	MORNAS	B	MORNAS
RELAIS	de	LANCON DE PROVENCE	A-B-C	LANCON DE PROVENCE

ON MOTORWAY A.10				
L'ARCHE	d'	ORLEANS	A-B-C	ORLEANS
L'ARCHE	de	TOURS	B	TOURS
L'ARCHE	de	CHATELLERAULT-Est	B	CHATELLERAULT
L'ARCHE	de	CHATELLERAULT-Ouest	B	CHATELLERAULT

ON MOTORWAY A.11				
L'ARCHE	de	CHARTRES-Sud	B	CHARTRES
L'ARCHE	de	CHARTRES-Nord	B	CHARTRES
L'ARCHE	de	LA FERTE BERNARD	B	LA FERTE BERNARD

ON MOTORWAY A.13				
L'ARCHE	de	VIRONVAY	B	ROUEN

ON MOTORWAY A.43				
L'ARCHE	de	L'ISLE D'ABEAU	A-B-C	L'ISLE D'ABEAU

This sign-logo reads:

KINDNESS, COURTESY, QUALITY.

So wherever you come across this sign; a restaurant, a hotel a garage, a car or any other place, it would be most likely th the implied connotation is precisely correct. It is in the interes of all of the users of this guide that the LE GUIDE sign displayed appropriately. Please help.

The actual Routes
of the Guide

(going south)

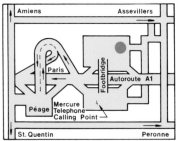
85

CALAIS

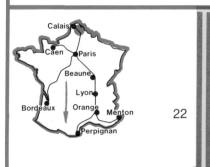

22

22

16

A26

St. Omer

38

Tic

13

ALL DISTANCES

IN

KILOMETRES

51

**YOU DRIVE
ON
THE RIGHT
HAND SIDE
OF
THE ROAD**

9

Unleaded petrol

60

Amiens,
Lilliers

13

73

(73)

Béthune

22

PORT

Aire de **Zutkerque**

WC

Newly built, very elegant.

SOS - actually on the rest area.

Aire de **Barrière de péage**

WC

Open space type of area with tables and benches, grassy, small and pleasant.

Aire du **Grand Riez**

WC

As above, climbing frame, lit.
SOS — at side of the Area.

Aire de **Rely**

Very open, spacious, lot of grassy spots, newly developed.
SOS — at the side.

Aire du **Reveillon**

WC

Enclosed, forested, tables and benches, some among trees, lit at night, climbing frame, very nice.
SOS — at the side.

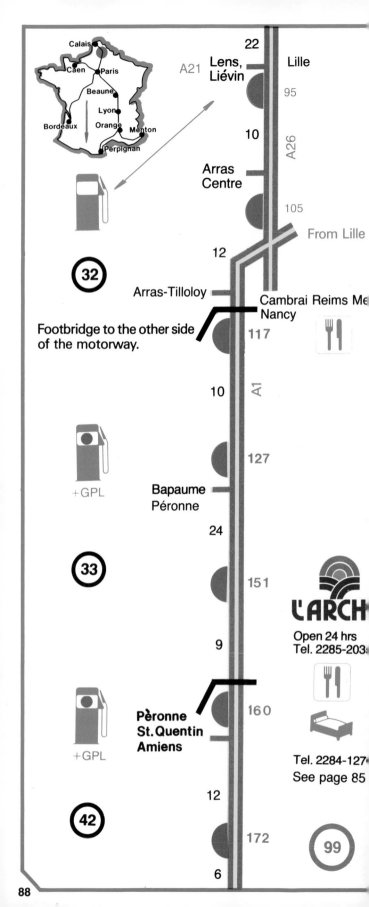

22

A21

Lens,
Liévin

Lille

95

10

A26

Arras
Centre

105

From Lille

(32)

12

Arras-Tilloloy

Cambrai Reims Me
Nancy

Footbridge to the other side
of the motorway.

117

10

A1

+GPL

127

Bapaume
Péronne

24

(33)

151

9

L'ARCH

Open 24 hrs
Tel. 2285-203

+GPL

160

Pèronne
St.Quentin
Amiens

Tel. 2284-127
See page 85

12

(42)

172

6

(99)

88

Aire de Souches

Just parking facilities. Small.
SOS — at side.

Aire des Trois Crettes

Open type with few tables and benches. Lit at night, spacious.
SOS — towards the exit.

Aire de Wancourt-Ouest

Open space type of area, few tables and benches, pleasant.

Aire de St. Léger

As above. Hot drinks available from dispensing machines.
SOS — located just before the entry to the Area.

Aire de Maurepas

Small with tables and benches, lit at night, grassy and nice
SOS — at the side.

Aire d'Assevillers

Ample parking facilities. Cafeteria, grill, boutique there is a footbridge to the other side of the m-way Rest Area.
SOS — at the side.

Aire d'Hattencourt

Open space type of area. Tables and benches. Nice.
SOS — at the side.

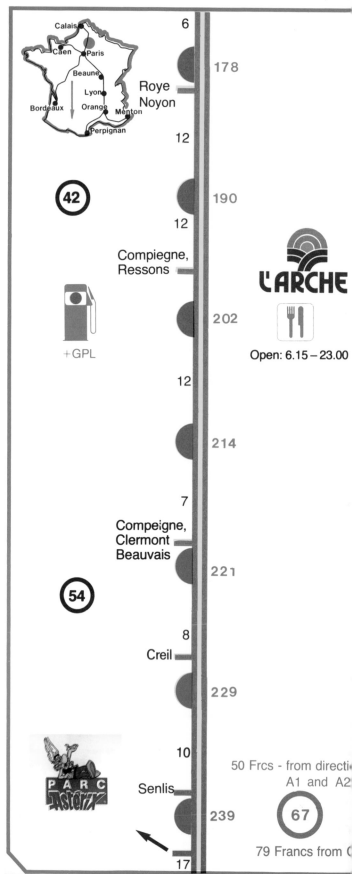

6
178

Roye
Noyon

12

42

190

12

Compiegne,
Ressons

+GPL

202

L'ARCHE

Open: 6.15 – 23.00

12

214

7

Compeigne,
Clermont
Beauvais

221

54

8

Creil

229

10

Senlis

239

50 Frcs - from directi
A1 and A2

67

79 Francs from C

17

Aire de Goyencourt-Ouest

There are tables and benches. Some of the sets are under cover. Nice.
SOS — towards the entry.

Aire de Tilolloy-Ouest

Plenty of tables and benches, most are among trees. Lit at night, climbing frames. Very nice.
SOS — at the side towards the exit.

Aire de Ressons-Ouest

Usual facilities of petrol station complex. The exit to Compiegne combined with the entrence to the Rest Area.
SOS - at the side close to the entry.

Aire de Bois d'Arsy

Spacious, tables and benches among trees and in the open space. Swings for children, climbing frames, lit. Nice.
SOS — towards the exit.

Aire de Longueil

Very small but nice, few tables and benches, some trees. Situated on a hill.
SOS — just past the Area

Aire de Roberval-Ouest

Tables and benches, some trees, very small area but pleasant.
SOS — at the entry.

Aire de Barrière de péage

Open space type of area. Exit for Senlis actually takes place at the "barrière de péage".

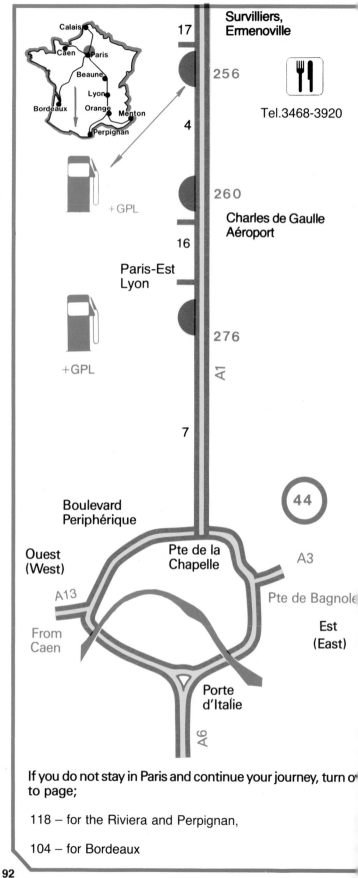

Survilliers,
Ermenoville

17

256

🍴

Tel.3468-3920

4

260

Charles de Gaulle
Aéroport

16

Paris-Est
Lyon

276

+GPL

A1

7

+GPL

44

Boulevard
Periphérique

Ouest
(West)

Pte de la
Chapelle

A3

A13

Pte de Bagnole

From
Caen

Est
(East)

Porte
d'Italie

A6

If you do not stay in Paris and continue your journey, turn o
to page;

118 – for the Riviera and Perpignan,

104 – for Bordeaux

Aire de Vemars

Wide selection of services. Self-service cefeteria and restaurant.
SOS - towards the entry.

Aire de Chennevières

There are tables and benches among trees, very tidy small. Pleasant.
SOS — not far from the exit.

Aire de la Courneuve

Limited services as indicated.
SOS — near the entrence to the Area.

ALTEA HOTEL ★★★
A.S.P.Darvault, Autoroute A6,
77140 — Nemours
Tel.6428-1032,Telex:690 243

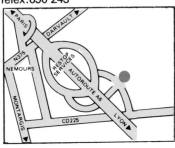

02 rooms with fully equipped bathroom ● radio ● TV ● telephone ● mini-bar ● motorway restaurants on near-by service area ● children play ground.

But now, having passed the Rest Area — Aire de Chennevieres and depending on, whether you stay in Paris or drive past you continue your journey as follows;-

You stay in Paris.

Since there are alternatives to follow,you need to decide upon your choice,depending on your intended destination in Paris

You may;

1. leave the motorway at the exit "Paris-Est, Lyon" and join the Boulevard Periphérique at the Pte de Bagnolet ("Pte" — short form for "Porte", which means "gate" in this particular instance)

2. drive straight on,and before reaching Pte de la Chapelle you follow;

— the sign "Pte de Clignancourt" if you want to go Ouest (West) or,

— if you want to go Est (East) you follow the sign 'Pte d'Aubervilliers" which is next to Pte de la Villette, the nearest, convenient location of one of the Arcade hotels just outside of the City of Science and Industry with it's famous now "GÉODE" — a unique spherical giant structure, housing one of the biggest hemispheric screens in the world, a "must" to visit when in Paris, or,

— straight on,following the sign "Paris".

You need to be equipped with a good map, covering Paris with its great majority of streets offering "one way" only traffic.

I take the opportunity here,to advise you to acquire the Michelin **PLAN DE PARIS** (blue cover, 1cm = 100 metres) and you will not get lost in Paris

You drive past Paris

Take the exit for "Paris-Est, Lyon" and at the next choice of alternatives take the route for "Paris-Sud",leading you to the Pte de Bagnolet, and continue along the Boleuvard Periphérique round Paris,until you reach the pte d'Italie at which it is necessary to leave the Boulevard for your journey to the Sun. Do not concentrate your attention on the Pte d'Italie and KEEP in lane for LYON.

If you miss the above mentioned exit for "Paris-Est, Lyon" you are still O.K. joining the Boulevard at the location of Pte de la Chapelle. Just before this Gate, you have 3 possibilities but must not take the Pte de la Chapelle, otherwise you will enter the City of Paris.

it happens, that you went straight on , turn round as soon
s you realize your error, and follow the sign ''Boulevard
eriphérique'' and then one of the two alternatives; ''EST'' -
ast or ''OUEST'' - West. Est seems to be the obvious choice
ut either will take you to the A1- Autoroute du Soleil if you
EEP in lane for LYON.

n the Boulevard Periphérique keep in lane, at least second
om the right hand side. The extreme right hand side lane
riving can easily lead to some frustration as the incoming
affic joins the Boulevard in a manner, as if, there was nobody
lse driving. But the "Priorite a droite" rule explains evrything.
ee "Tips Plus" chapter for further comments.

you are heading for Bordeaux, you should follow the same
oute as for LYON until you have left the Boulevard and come
cross a choice for ''Lyon'' and ''Chartres, Orleans''.

you happen to drive for Bordeaux using the western part
f the Boulevard you may be tempted to take an earlier exit
or Orleans. Unless you know the route well, do not try it if
me is of importance. It is apparent that on the way you have
o go through local traffic.

the immediate vicinity of Pte d'Italie you will face awkward,
mall radius bends entering into suddenly darkened tunnels.
ake care.

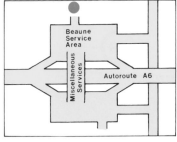

CAEN

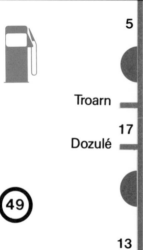

	5
	5
Troarn	A13
	17
Dozulé	
	2 2
(49)	
	13
	35
Deauville	Gend
	19

11 Fr

(35)

PULLMAN GRAND HOTEL * * * *de Luxe

Promenade Marcel — Proust,
14390 — Cabourg

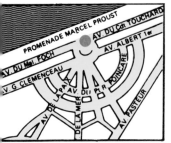

Tel.3191-0179,

Telex: 171364

rooms and suites ● bathroom ● colour TV ● radio ● telephone ●
restaurant ● piano ● bar ● reception — conference rooms ●
numerous sport facilities ● City swimming pool close to hotel ●
parking facilities ● direct access to the beach.

REMEMBER

**YOU DRIVE ON THE RIGHT
HAND SIDE OF THE ROAD**

Aire Sud de Giberville

Spacious, grassy area.
SOS — at the side.

Aire de Barrière de péage

Just parking spaces. Very small.

Aire de Beaumont

Small, grassy. Some trees, tables and benches, very pretty.
Recommended.
SOS — just past the Rest Area.

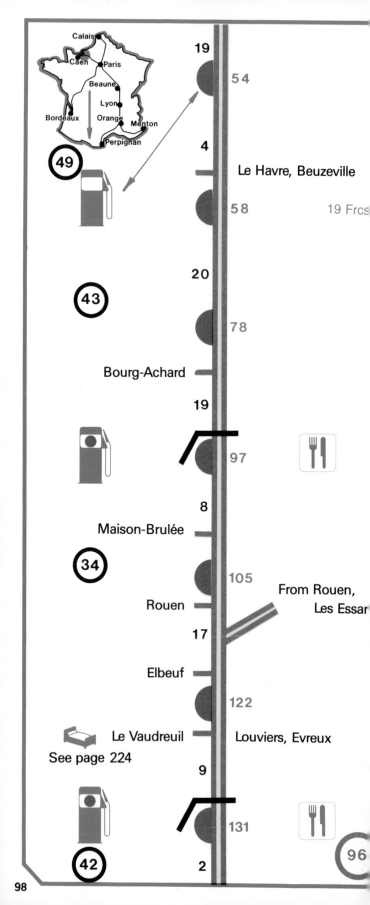

Calais
Caen Paris
Beaune
Lyon
Bordeaux Orange
Menton
Perpignan

49

19

54

4

Le Havre, Beuzeville

58

19 Frcs

20

43

78

Bourg-Achard

19

97

8

Maison-Brulée

34

105

Rouen

From Rouen,
Les Essar

17

Elbeuf

122

Le Vaudreuil
See page 224

Louviers, Evreux

9

42

131

96

2

Aire Sud de Beuzeville

Spacious, some tables and benches, grassy, pleasant.
SOS — located toward exit.

Aire de Barrière de péage

Very small with few parking spaces. More sort of a parking bay.

Aire du Moulin

Small with tables and benches, very nice.
SOS — just past the Rest Area.

Aire de Bosgouet

Just parking facilities. Snack-bar.
SOS — just past the Area.
Info-Route.

Aire Sud de Robert-le-Diable

SOS — by the side, towards the end of the Rest Area.
Located actually on the Area, not easy to spot from the Motorway.

Aire Sud de Bord

There are tables and benches among trees.
SOS — at the side of Area.

Aire de Vironvay

Spacious in parking facilities. Interconnected with the other side of Rest Area. Cafeteria.
SOS — at the side of Area.

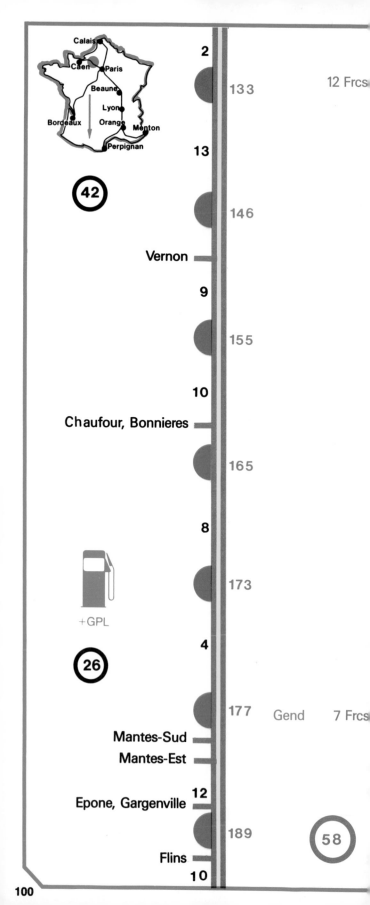

2

133

12 Frcs

13

42

146

Vernon

9

155

10

Chaufour, Bonnieres

165

8

+GPL

173

4

26

177   Gend   7 Frcs

Mantes-Sud
Mantes-Est

12

Epone, Gargenville

189   58

Flins

10

100

Aire de Barrière de péage

SOS — not far, having passed the Area.

Aire Sud de Beauchene

Partly forested. Tables and benches.
SOS — at the entry to the Area.

Aire Sud de Douains

Very basic, just parking spaces.
SOS — at the side of Area.

Aire Sud de la Villeneuve en Chevrie

Small, arranged at two levels. There are few tables and
benches among trees at the upper level.
SOS — at the side.

Aire de Rosny-sur-Seine

Few tables and benches, generaly parking spaces.
SOS — at the side of Area.

Aire de Barrière de péage

Just parking facilities. Gendarmerie.

NO NAME -Rest Area

SOS — not far from the exit,past the Rest Area.

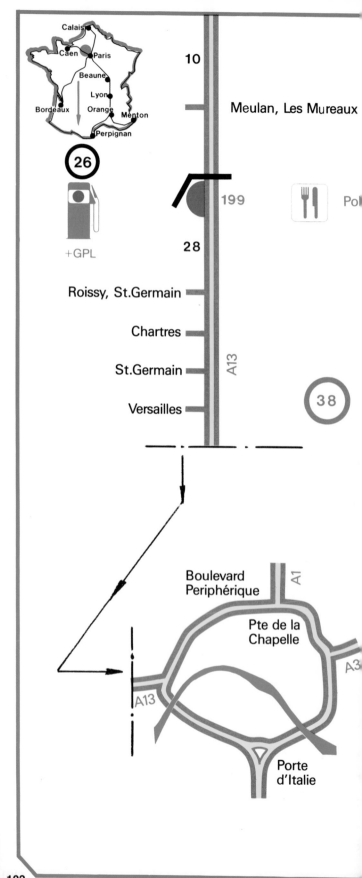

Aire Sud de Morainvilliers

Ample Rest Area, footbridge to the other side of
Motorway Rest Area

you do not stay in Paris and continue your journey to the
outh, turn over to page ;-

18 – for the Riviera and Perpignan,

04 – for Bordeaux

ake "Paris-Sud" before joining Boulevard Periphérique and
ollow the sign "Lyon" whether you go for Bordeaux or the
iviera.
ead further comments on page 78 and 79.

you go for Bordeaux, you may opt for an earlier exit for
hartres which leads to the Autoroute A10 but the details are
ot available for this edition.

ARCADE HOTEL PORTSMOUTH

Winston Churchill Avenue
Portsmouth PO1 2DG
Tel. (0705) 821 992, Telex: 869 429

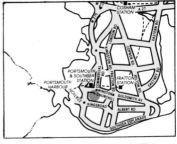

4 modern rooms with WC and shower ● telephone ● TV on
quest ● automatic morning call ● restaurant ● bar ● 3 conference
oms ● situated in the town centre, covenient for the continental
rry port ● private car park

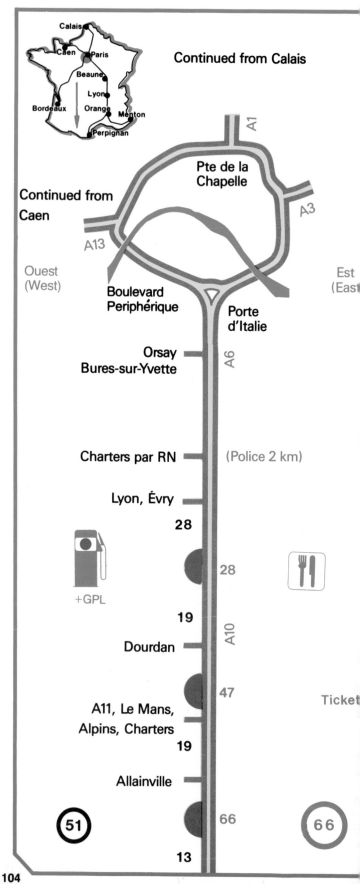

Continued from Calais

Pte de la Chapelle

A1

A3

Continued from Caen

A13

Ouest (West)

Est (East)

Boulevard Periphérique

Porte d'Italie

Orsay
Bures-sur-Yvette

A6

Charters par RN

(Police 2 km)

Lyon, Évry

28

28

+GPL

19

A10

Dourdan

47

A11, Le Mans, Alpins, Charters

19

Ticket

Allainville

51

66

66

13

L'ARCHE RESTAURANTS

Aire de **Limours-Janvry**

Just parking spaces. Cafeteria, currency exchange at the cash desk.
SOS at the side.

Aire de **Barrière de péage**

Few tables and benches. Pleasant.

Aire de **Boutroux**

Spacious with some tables and benches, grassy, small trees, interesting.

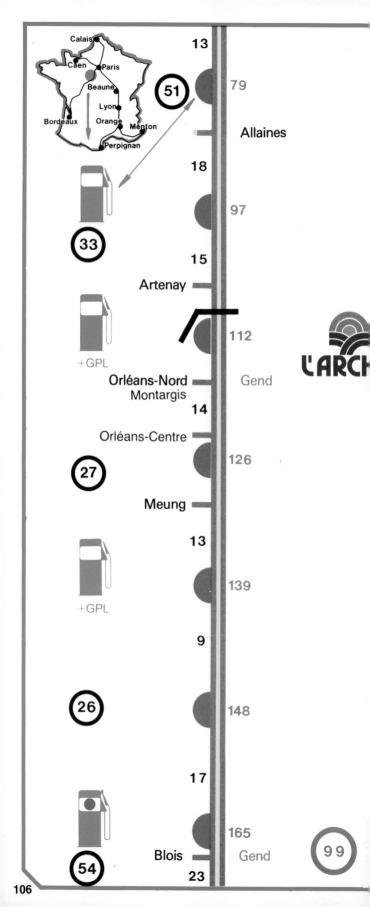

13

51

79

Allaines

18

33

97

15

Artenay

112

Orléans-Nord   Gend
Montargis

14

Orléans-Centre

27

126

Meung

+GPL

13

139

9

26

148

17

54

165

Blois   Gend   99

23

L'ARCH

ire de Francheville

ar, buffet, boutique.
OS - 100 m past the area.

ire du Héron-Cendré

pacious, jungle-like with tables and benches.
OS - at the side.

Aire d' Orléans-Saran

ar, grill, boutique. Footbridge to the other side of the
motorway Service Area.
OS — at the side. Info-Route

Aire de Bellevue

WC

OS at the side of the Area.

Aire de Meung-Sur-Loire

few tables and benches. Pleasant.
OS — at some distance from the entry.

Aire des Fougeres

WC

Open type of area, a lot of tables and benches in a row.
Pleasant.
OS — at the side.

Aire de Blois-Villerbon

Cafeteria, bar.
OS — not far from exit.

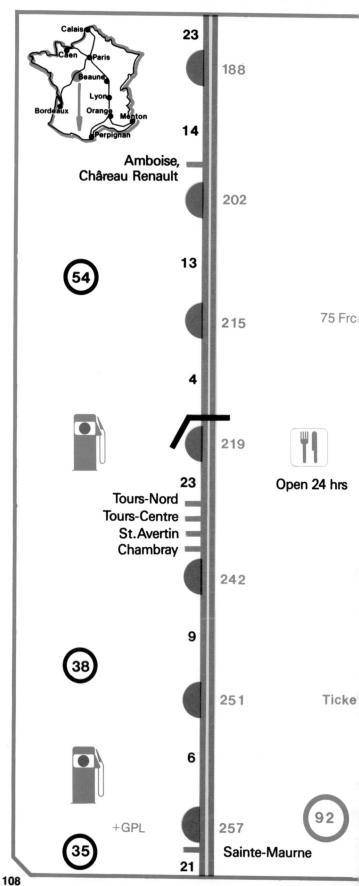

Calais
Caen Paris
Beaune
Lyon
Bordeaux Orange
Menton
Perpignan

23

188

14

Amboise,
Châreau Renault

202

(54)

13

215

75 Fra

4

219

Open 24 hrs

23

Tours-Nord
Tours-Centre
St.Avertin
Chambray

242

9

(38)

251

Ticke

6

+GPL

257

(92)

(35)

Sainte-Maurne

21

Aire de la Chatière

Tables and benches in the open and among trees. Small and pleasant.
SOS — 300 m past the Area.

Aire de la Courte Epée

Forested, a lot of tables and benches.

Aire de Barrière de péage

Open type area. Few tables and benches.
SOS — 300 m from the entry.

Aire de Tours-La Longue-Vue

Interconnected by a footbridge. There are; Bar, buffet, boutique, sandwich bar.
SOS — at the exit end.

Aire du Village-Brule

Forested with a lot of tables and benches. Spacious.
SOS — at the side.

Aire de Barrière de péage

There are some tables and benches.

Aire de St.Maure de Touraine

SOS — at the side of Area.

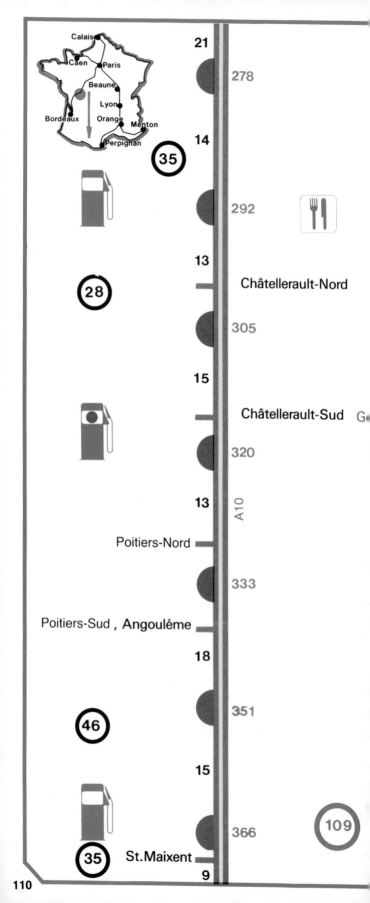

21

278

14

35

28

13

292

Châtellerault-Nord

305

15

Châtellerault-Sud   G

320

A10

13

Poitiers-Nord

333

Poitiers-Sud , Angouléme

18

351

46

15

366

109

35   St.Maixent

9

Aire de Maille

Forested with a lot of tables and benches. Very pleasant.
SOS — at the entry to Area.

Aire de Chatellerault Antran

Just parking facilities.

SOS - at side of the area.

Aire des Meuniers

Forested, tables and benches, spacious and smart.

SOS — at the side of the Area.

Aire de Poitiers Jaunay-Clan

SOS — at the side of the Area.

Aire des Gent-Saptiers

Open type, tables and benches. Pleasant.
SOS — at the side.

Aire de Coulombiers-Nord

Open type, some trees, lit at night, tables and benches. Nice.
SOS — at the entry.

Aire de Rouillé-Pamproux

Take care at the entry — small radius bend. Take first one on
the right hand side. Tables and benches, it is very nice indeed.
SOS — at the side. Info-Route

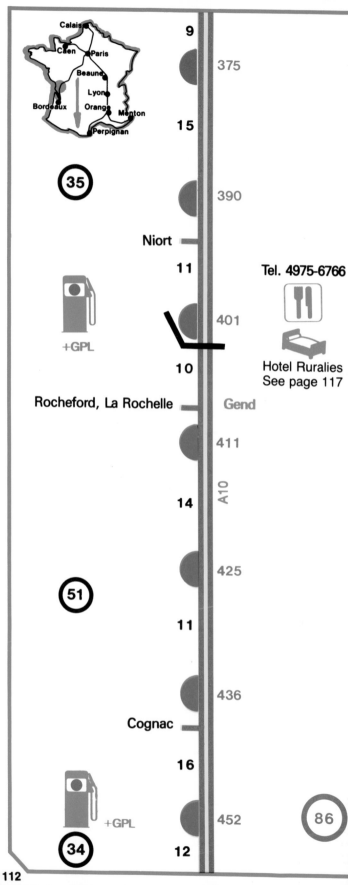

9

375

15

35

390

Niort

11

Tel. 4975-6766

401

+GPL

Hotel Ruralies
See page 117

10

Rocheford, La Rochelle

Gend

411

14

A10

425

51

11

436

Cognac

16

+GPL

452

34

12

86

Aire de Ste Eanne-Nord

Open type of area, swings, tables and benches. Very nice.
SOS — at the side towards exit.

Aire de Ste Néomaye-Nord

Open type space. Lit at night, swings, tables and benches.
Rather small. Recommended.
SOS — at the side.

Aire des Les Ruralies

Tables and benches. Interconnected with the other side. Very complex Area. Museum, strongly recommended.
SOS - at the side. Info-Route.

Aire de Gript-Nord

Open type space, tables and benches. Very nice.
SOS — at the side towards the entry.

Aire de Doeuil s/le Mignon

Quite spacious with tables and benches. Very pleasant.
SOS — at the exit end.

Aire de Lozay

Tables and benches, swings, rocking things. Lit at night, open space area, spacious.
SOS — at side, towards the entry.

Aire de Fenioux

Spacious, open space area, tables and benches. Lit at night, swings, climbing nets. Nice.
SOS — at the side.

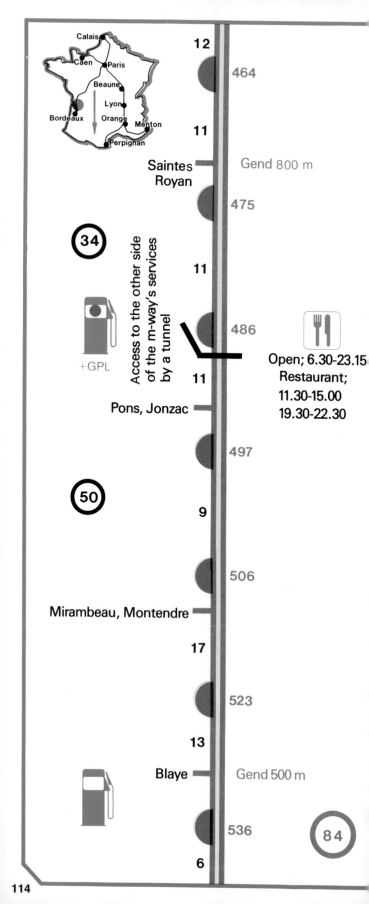

12

464

11

Gend 800 m

Saintes
Royan

475

(34)

11

Access to the other side
of the m-way's services
by a tunnel

486

+GPL

Open; 6.30-23.15
Restaurant;
11.30-15.00
19.30-22.30

11

Pons, Jonzac

497

(50)

9

506

Mirambeau, Montendre

17

523

13

Blaye

Gend 500 m

536

(84)

6

Aire de Port d'Envaux

In two parts; open space and forested. Tables and benches.
Rather nice.
SOS — at the side by the entry.

Aire de Chermignac

Open space type of area with tables and benches.
SOS — at the side of Area.

Aire de St-Léger

Very spacious, picnicking-area, tables and benches. Swings
climbing frames. Very elegant, recommended.
SOS — at the exit end.

Aire de St-Palais

Tables and benches among trees and in the open. Small tidy
and very nice.
SOS — not far from the entry.

Aire de St.Ciers

Tables and benches among trees and in the open space. Lit
at night, spacious, very pleasant. Recommended.
SOS — at the side, near the entry.

Aire de St.Cabrais

Tables and benches among trees and in the open space. Lit
at night.
SOS — at the side of Area.

Aire de Saugon

As above. Recommended.
SOS — at the side. Info-Route.

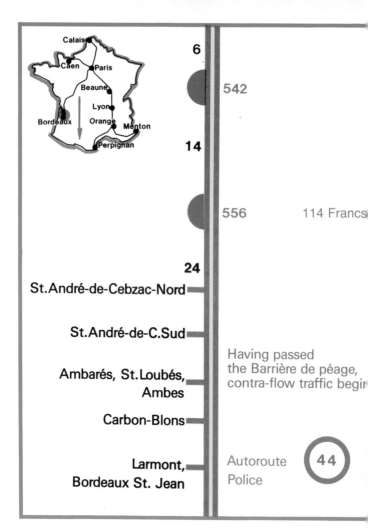

	6	
		542
	14	
		556	114 Francs
	24	
St.André-de-Cebzac-Nord		
St.André-de-C.Sud		
Ambarés, St.Loubés, Ambes		Having passed the Barrière de péage, contra-flow traffic begin
Carbon-Blons		
Larmont, Bordeaux St. Jean		Autoroute Police (44)

BORDEAUX

PULLMAN HOTEL ★★★★
Quartier Meriadeck, 5 Rue R — Lateulade,
33000 — Bordeaux
Tel.5690-9237, Telex:540565

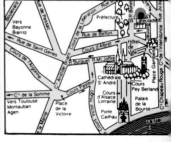

196 rooms ● details page 14 ● TV with video circuit ● restaurant
bar ● parking ● a large hotel in the centre of Bordeaux 12 km from
Bordeaux — Merignac airport.

Aire de **St.Christoly**

Tables and benches among trees and in the open space.
Spacious. Recommended.
SOS — at the entry.

Aire de **Barrière de péage**

Just parking spaces.

WELCOME TO RURALIES

The Product stocked in the shop **La Vitrine des Produits Regionaux** have been selected by the regional committee, a guarantee for you of their origin and quality.

They are offered directly to you for sale by the producers of Poitou-Charentes, thus ensuring, you will be able to buy the best wines, cognac, pineau and many other goods from our area.

HOTEL LES RURALIES **

Aotoroute A10, Aire d'Aiffres-Vouille,
79230 – Prahecq.
Tel.4975-6766, Telex:793 553 Ruralie, Fax. 4975-8029.

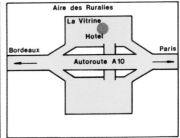

0 rooms with bathrooms ● TV with satelite system ● rooms for disabled people ● direct telephone ● restaurante - regional cuisune ● Self service ● conference rooms ● direct access from both sides of the motorway ● possibility of return journey without leaving the motorway.

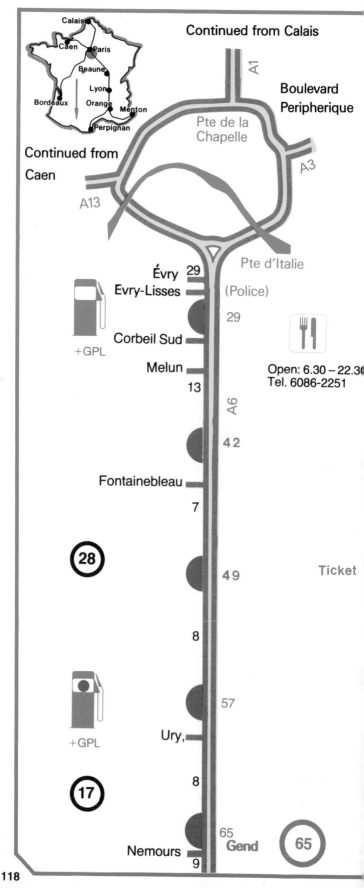

Continued from Calais

A1

Boulevard
Peripherique

Pte de la
Chapelle

A3

Continued from
Caen

A13

Pte d'Italie

Évry 29
Evry-Lisses

(Police)

29

Corbeil Sud

Melun

13

A6

42

Fontainebleau

7

(28)

49

Ticket

8

+GPL

57

(17)

Ury,

8

65
Gend

(65)

Nemours

9

Open: 6.30 – 22.30
Tel. 6086-2251

Aire de Lisses

Just parking facilicies. Cafeteria, boutique. Combined entry to te Rest Area with the exit from the m-way. SOS — at side.

Aire de Nainville

Forested, tables and benches among trees. Small but nice. SOS - on the parking area.

Aire de Barrière de péage

Just parking facilities. Spacious.

Aire d'Achères la Foret

There are tables and benches.
Well stocked shop with maps & guides.
SOS - located at side of area.

Aire de Villiers

Very nice woodland type of area. There are tables and benches. Spacious. First best.
SOS — actually on the Rest Area at the very end, difficult to be spotted from the motorway.

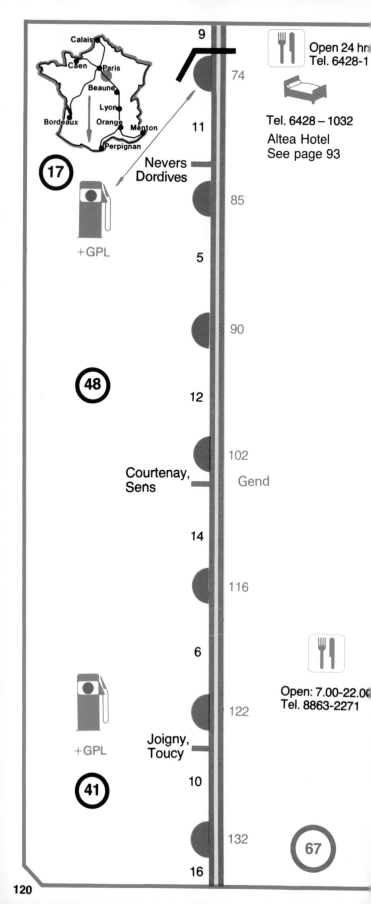

9

74

Open 24 hrs
Tel. 6428-1

11

Tel. 6428 – 1032
Altea Hotel
See page 93

17

+GPL

Nevers
Dordives

85

5

90

48

12

102

Courtenay,
Sens

Gend

14

116

6

Open: 7.00-22.00
Tel. 8863-2271

122

+GPL

Joigny,
Toucy

41

10

132

67

16

Aire de Nemours

Ample services provided, typical for petrol station complex. Few tables and benches, interconnected with the other side of the m-way Rest Area.
SOS — at the side. Info-Route.

Aire de Sonville

Small, but very nice. Forested and partly open area. Plenty of tables and benches.
SOS — at the side.

Aire du Liard

Forested, tables and benches, very nice. Partly open space.
SOS — at side.

Aire du Parc Thierry

It is a jungle type of area with plenty of tables and benches among the trees obviously.
SOS — towards the exit.

Aire des Chataigniers

Large, jungle like type, as above. Very nice.
SOS — at side.

Aire de la Réserve

Open space arranged just for parking. There is a bar, buffet, cafeteria.
SOS — at side.

Aire de la Racheuse

Forested area. Small with tables and benches.
SOS.

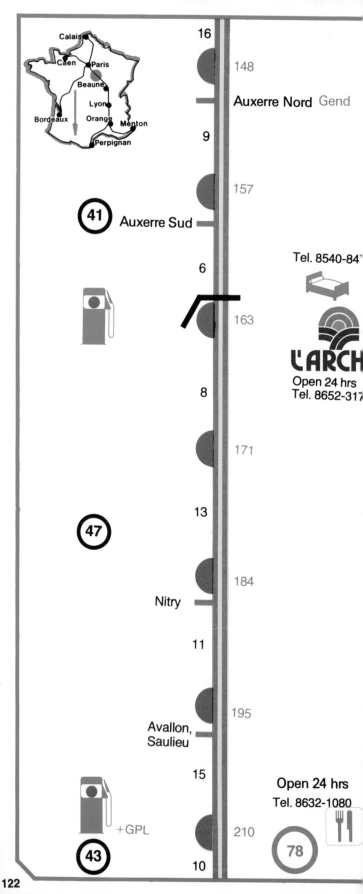

16

148

Auxerre Nord Gend

9

157

(41) Auxerre Sud

6

Tel. 8540-84

163

L'ARCH

Open 24 hrs
Tel. 8652-317

8

171

13

(47)

184

Nitry

11

195

Avallon,
Saulieu

15

Open 24 hrs
Tel. 8632-1080

+GPL

210

(78)

(43)

10

Aire de la Biche

Forested area but no tables or benches provided. Nice.
SOS — at side.

Aire des Bois Impériaux Courte Epée

Small with tables and benches.
SOS — at the side by the exit.

Aire de Venoy Grosse Pierre

Very spacious, few tables and benches, footbridge to the
other side of motorway. Bar, self-service, stamps at the
boutique. Collection 9.10 a.m. letter box by the cafeteria.
SOS — towards the entry.

Aire de la Grosse Tour

Very small with tables and benches. In two parts; forested
and open space. Nice.

Aire de la Couée

Small, forested with tables and benches. Nice.
SOS — at the entry.

Aire de Montmorency

Forested, a lot of tables and benches.
SOS — 400 m past the Area.

Aire de la Chaponne

Just parking spaces. Grill, self-service.
SOS — at the side.

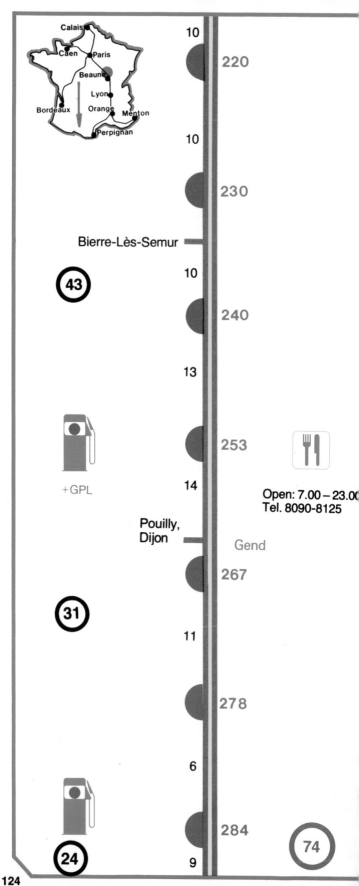

10

220

10

230

Bierre-Lès-Semur

43

10

240

13

+GPL

253

14

Open: 7.00 – 23.00
Tel. 8090-8125

Pouilly,
Dijon

Gend

267

31

11

278

6

284

24

9

74

Aire d' Epoisses

Open type area, tables and benches. Very nice, recommended.
SOS — at side.

Aire de Ruffey

Open type and grassy area. No tables nor benches.
SOS – by the entry.

Aire de Fermenot

Spacious with tables and benches among trees. Nice.
SOS — at the entry.

Aire du Chien Blanc

Open space , very spacious, newly arranged, very modern, tidy and very nice. There are tables and benches. Recommended.
SOS — at side.

Aire de Chaignot

There are tables and benches among trees. Jungle like.
SOS — at side.

Aire de la Garenne

Pleasant, situated on the side of a hill with a panoramic view. Tables and benches.

SOS – at the side, close to the entry.

Aire de la Forêt

Very spacious, which is not apparant at first. Located beyond the petrol station.
SOS — at side.

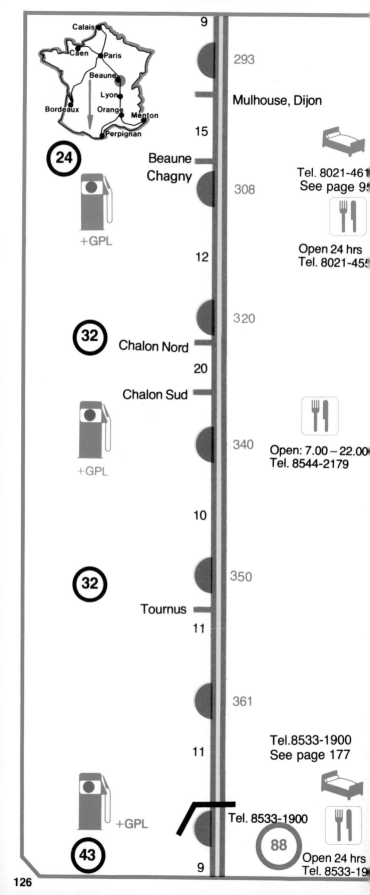

9

293

Mulhouse, Dijon

15

24

+GPL

Beaune
Chagny

308

Tel. 8021-461
See page 9?

Open 24 hrs
Tel. 8021-455

12

320

32

Chalon Nord

20

Chalon Sud

+GPL

340

Open: 7.00 – 22.00
Tel. 8544-2179

10

32

350

Tournus

11

361

11

Tel.8533-1900
See page 177

+GPL

Tel. 8533-1900

43

88

9

Open 24 hrs
Tel. 8533-19

Aire du Rossignol

Small and pleasant, woodland type, there are tables and benches and some grassy spots.
SOS — by the entry.

Aire de Beaune Tailly

There is THE ARCHEODROME. Tel. 8021-4825 open throughout the year from 10.00 a.m. to 8.00 p.m. (May-Sept) and 10.00 a.m.- 6.00 p.m.(Oct.- Apr.)
SOS — at side.

Aire de le Curney

There is an impressive Memorial to the victims of the "Beaune" accident 31 July, 1982. See page 128. Spacious and forested, tables and benches.
SOS — at side.

Aire de la Ferté

Just car spaces provided. There is a bar and a buffet.
SOS — at side.

Aire de Jugy

Open space type type of area, small and pretty. There are tables and benches.
SOS — at side.

Aire de Farges

WC

As above.
SOS — at side.

Aire de Mâcon St. Albain

Spacious. Some tables and benches. Typical services for a petrol station complex. Cafeteria. Grill, bar.
SOS — by the entry.

THE BEAUNE MEMORIAL TO

Stop here for a moment, and try to comprehend the content of these pages. Think for a while and pay your respects to those killed and injured in road accidents.

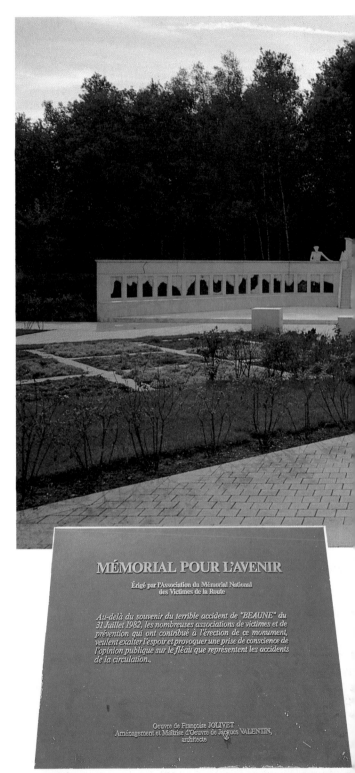

MÉMORIAL POUR L'AVENIR

Érigé par l'Association du Mémorial National
des Victimes de la Route

Au-delà du souvenir du terrible accident de "BEAUNE" du 31 Juillet 1982, les nombreuses associations de victimes et de prévention qui ont contribué à l'érection de ce monument, veulent exalter l'espoir et provoquer une prise de conscience de l'opinion publique sur le fléau que représentent les accidents de la circulation.

Oeuvre de Françoise JOLIVET
Aménagement et Maîtrise d'Oeuvre de Jacques VALENTIN,
architecte

o do so validates the purpose of this memorial and will help
s all to enjoy accident free holidays.

MEMORIAL FOR THE FUTURE

rected by the National Memorial Association for Road
Victims.

To go further than the memory of the dreadful accident near
Beaune on the 31st July, 1982, the many associations for
ictims and road safety who contributed to this memorial
wish to inspire hope and stimulate the conscience of public
pinion against the scourge which traffic accidents have
ecome."

And if you translate the word "scourge" into the likely
neaning of the word, "barbarian conquerers", this would
xactly mean what traffic accidents have become.

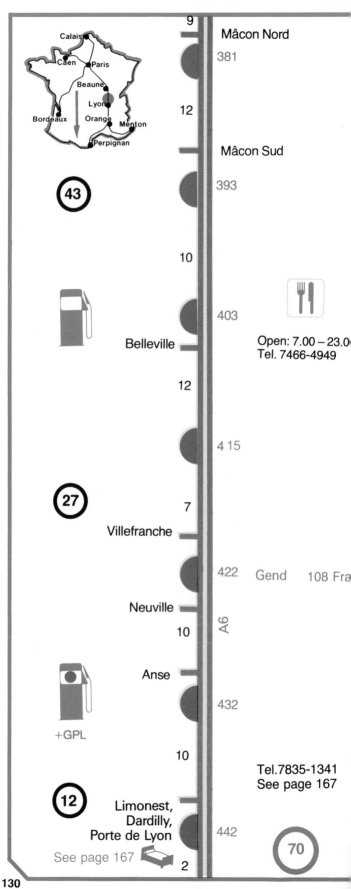

9

Mâcon Nord

381

12

Mâcon Sud

(43)

393

10

403

Belleville

Open: 7.00 – 23.0
Tel. 7466-4949

12

4 15

(27)

7

Villefranche

422   Gend   108 Fra

Neuville

A6

10

Anse

432

+GPL

10

Tel.7835-1341
See page 167

(12)

Limonest,
Dardilly,
Porte de Lyon

442

See page 167

2

(70)

Aire de Sennecé

Small and smart.
SOS — at side.

Aire de Crèches

Open space type of area, nests of tables and stools or benches, very modern. Attractive.
SOS — at the side.

Aire de Dracé

Open space, tables and benches, lot of grassy area, pleasant. Restaurant, cafeteria.
SOS — at the entry.

Aire de Patural

Very small with tables and benches. Very open. Pleasant.
SOS — by the entry.

Aire de Barrière de péage

Just parking spaces. In the stage of development.
Gendarmerie

Aire des Chêres

Spacious, open type of area with tables and benches.
Picnic site, just past the main service complex.
SOS — at side.

Porte de Lyon, Limonest, Dardilly

The same, exit slip road.
There is an impressive nest of many hotels and a camping site and a petrol station with a very well stocked shop.
Petrol is priced very competitively. It is not a Rest Area

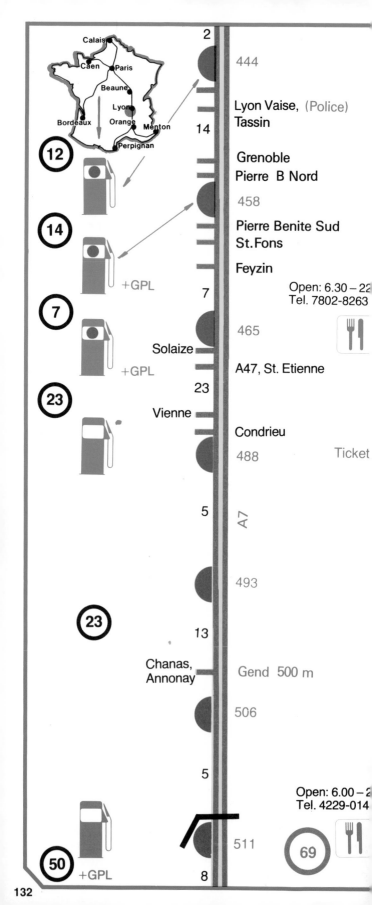

2

444

Lyon Vaise, (Police)
Tassin

14

Grenoble
Pierre B Nord

458

Pierre Benite Sud
St. Fons

Feyzin

Open: 6.30 – 22
Tel. 7802-8263

7

465

Solaize

A47, St. Etienne

23

Vienne

Condrieu

488

Ticket

5

A7

493

13

Chanas,
Annonay

Gend 500 m

506

5

Open: 6.00 – 2
Tel. 4229-014

511

69

8

Aire de Dardilly

Just parking facilities.
SOS — at side.

Aire de Pierre Bénite Nord

As above. Exit for Pierre Benite and entry to the Rest Area is combined.
SOS — just before entry.

Aire de Solaize

As above. Spacious.

Aire de Barrière de péage

As above. Info-Route.

Aire d' Auberives

Pique-nique jeux d'enfants area. Best so far. (Suitable for parties with young children). Lit at night.
SOS — at side.

Aire de Chanas

No facilities. Very small, few tables.
SOS — at side.

Aire de St. Rambert d'Albon

Pique-nique area, tables and benches. Very pretty with attractive type of trees. Footbridge to the other side of the motorway. Recommended.
SOS — at side. Info-route.

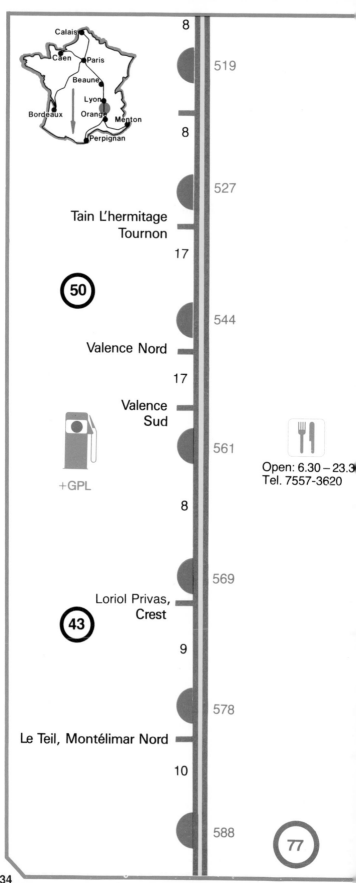

8

519

8

527

Tain L'hermitage
Tournon

17

(50)

544

Valence Nord

17

Valence
Sud

561

+GPL

Open: 6.30 – 23.3
Tel. 7557-3620

8

569

Loriol Privas,
Crest

(43)

9

578

Le Teil, Montélimar Nord

10

588

(77)

Aire de Blacheronde

Very small, few benches, some trees. Pleasant.
SOS – at side by the entry.

Aire du Bornaron

Pique-nique jeux d'enfants. Large, very nice.
Recommended.
SOS — at side.

Aire de Pont de l'Isère

Very small, grassy with tables and benches.
Recommended.
SOS – not far from the entry.

Aire de Portes-Lès-Valence

Pique-nique jeux d'enfants. There are tables and benches,
average.
SOS – actually on the rest area. Info-Route.

Aire de Bellevue

Very small with nests of tables and stools, some trees,
attractive.
SOS — by the entry.

Aire de Bras de Zil

Rather spacious with attractive trees, there are tables and
benches. Very pretty. Recommended.
SOS — at side.

Aire de la Coucourde

Pique-nique jeux d'enfants, very spacious, forested and
grassy. Attractive.
SOS — just past the Area.

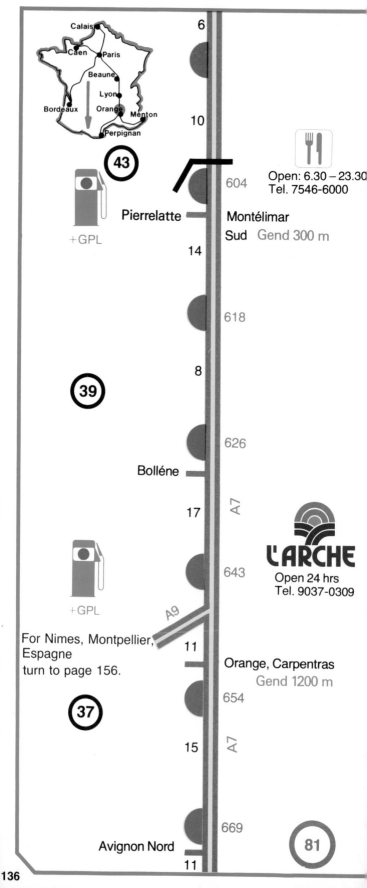

6

43

+GPL

Pierrelatte

10

604

Montélimar
Sud   Gend 300 m

Open: 6.30 – 23.30
Tel. 7546-6000

14

618

39

8

626

Bolléne

17

A7

643

L'ARCHE
Open 24 hrs
Tel. 9037-0309

+GPL

A9

For Nimes, Montpellier,
Espagne
turn to page 156.

11

Orange, Carpentras
Gend 1200 m

37

654

15

A7

669

81

Avignon Nord

11

136

Aire de Savasse

Open type of area, tables and benches. Very elegant area.

SOS – 400 past the area.

Aire de Montélimar

Pique-nique jeux d'enfants. It is quite a forest. There is a bar ,grill, cafeteria, self-service. Interconnected. Attractive.
SOS — at side. Info-Route.

Aire de Pierrelatte

Small, open type of area with some trees. There are tables and benches. Attractive.
SOS – 400 m before the entry.

Aire du Bois des Lots

Very small but pleasant. There are tables and benches. Lit at night.
SOS — at the entry.

Aire de Mornas-Village

Average, self-service, grill. Few tables and benches.
SOS — at side.
Info-Route.

Aire d' Orange Le Grès

Pique-nique jeux d'enfants.
SOS — at side, actually on the are.

Aire du Fournalet

Pique-nique jeux d'enfants, rather small area.

SOS - on the rest area.

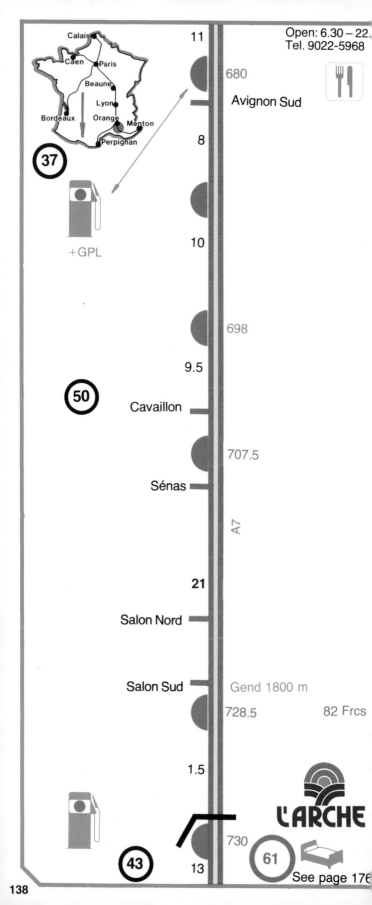

Open: 6.30 – 22.
Tel. 9022-5968

11
680
Avignon Sud

37
+GPL

8

10

698

9.5

50
Cavaillon

707.5
Sénas

A7

21
Salon Nord

Salon Sud   Gend 1800 m
728.5   82 Frcs

1.5

730
43   13   61
L'ARCHE
See page 176

138

Aire de Morières

Pique-nique jeux d'enfants. Hot & cold drinks from automatic machines, stereos, toys, magazines, good selection of maps and guides, wide range of car accessories, tee-shirts.

Aire de Cabannes

Very small, open space type of area, few benches. Lit.
SOS — a few hundred metres past the Area.

Aire de Cavaillon

As above, tables and benches. Nice.
SOS — at side.

Aire de Sénas

Small, open space, tables and benches and rather elegant.
SOS — at side.

Aire de Barrière de péage

As above. In a stage of development.

Aire de Lançon de Provence

There are tables and benches. Interconnected. Attractive
SOS — at side. Info-Route.

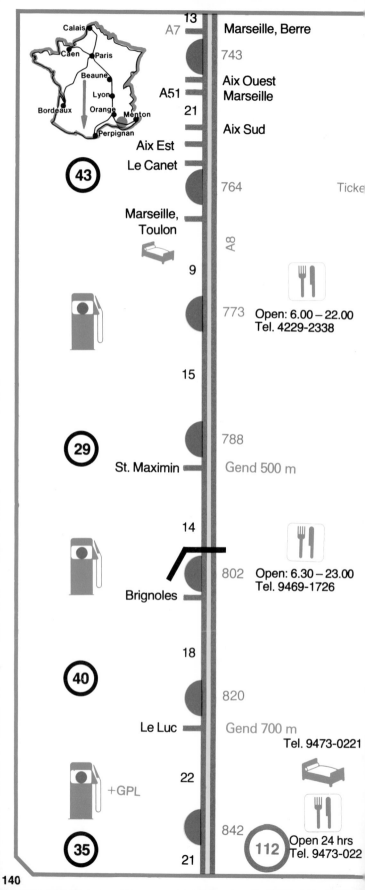

13
A7
Marseille, Berre

743

Aix Ouest Marseille

A51
21

Aix Sud

Aix Est
Le Canet

43

764   Ticke

Marseille, Toulon

A8

9

773   Open: 6.00 – 22.00
      Tel. 4229-2338

15

29

788

St. Maximin   Gend 500 m

14

802   Open: 6.30 – 23.00
      Tel. 9469-1726

Brignoles

18

40

820

Le Luc   Gend 700 m

Tel. 9473-0221

22

+GPL

842

35

112   Open 24 hrs
      Tel. 9473-022

21

Aire de Ventabren-Sud

Pique-nique jeux d'enfants.
SOS - 400 m before the entry.

Aire de Barrière de péage

Just parking facilities.

Aire de l' Ark

Very spacious but just parking facilities.
SOS - at the side.

Aire de Barcelonne

Tables and benches under cover. Very pretty.
SOS — at side.

Aire de Brignoles-Cambarette

Interconnected by a tunnel. Just parking facilities.
SOS — at side,

Aire de Roudal

Sited on the side of a hill, rather spacious and pleasant.
Recommended.
SOS at side by the entry.

Aire de Vidauban-Sud

Just parking facilities. Cafeteria.
SOS — at the side by the entry.

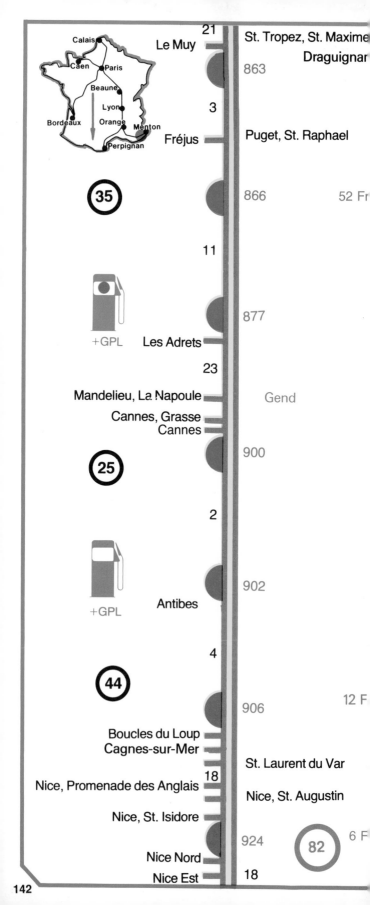

St. Tropez, St. Maxime
Draguignan
863
Le Muy
21

Fréjus
3
Puget, St. Raphael

35
866
52 Fr

11

+GPL
877
Les Adrets

23
Mandelieu, La Napoule
Gend
Cannes, Grasse
Cannes
900

25

2

+GPL
902
Antibes

4

44
906
12 F

Boucles du Loup
Cagnes-sur-Mer

St. Laurent du Var
18
Nice, Promenade des Anglais

Nice, St. Augustin

Nice, St. Isidore
924
82
6 F

Nice Nord
18
Nice Est

Aire du Jas Pellicot

Tables and benches, exotic trees, handsome Reast Area.
Lit.
SOS — at side.

Aire de Barrière de péage

Just parking spaces. Gendarmerie Station.
SOS actually on the rest area.

Aire de l' Esterel

Sited on a hill, very elegant with slides, swings, towers
climbing frame. Tables and benches. Recommended.
SOS – just past the exit from the area.

Aire de Belvedere du Piccoloret

Very open type of area, sited on the side of a hill. Nice
panoramic view. Lot of tables and benches.

Aire des Bréguières

Sited on a hill, forested, tables and benches, smart. There
is an Automobile Museum.

Aire de Barrière de péage

Just parking facilities.

Aire de Barrière de péage

Apparent lack of facilities.

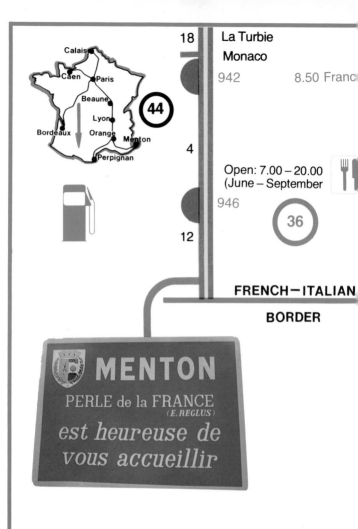

L'Office Municipal de Tourisme de la Ville de Menton would like attract your attention with the following invitation;

WELCOME TO MENTON
Right at the heart of the French/Italian Riviera lies the town Menton, always ready to receive tourists from all over the world.

This invitation is aimed primarily at the new comers to Fran as the tourists who have once visited Menton, come here tin and again and enjoy the unique atmosphere of this place. It located 25 km from Nice, 30 km San Remo, 7km Monaco, hours (door to door) flight from Paris due to the closeness the Nice/Cote d'Azur International Airport and 10 hours fro Paris by motorway. The 60 hotels ranging from 1 to 4 - st ratings are ready to make your stay in Menton memorable

The bay of Menton is world famous for its beauty. outstandingly temperate climate makes it the mildest Europe (300 sunny days a year).

Aire de **Barrière de péage**

As above.

Aire de **Beausoleil**

Sited on the side of a hill, by the Sea, very nice, modern with a panoramic view of Monaco.
SOS — just before entry.

The old districts overlooking the harbours and beaches ensure Menton has kept its style and pleasant life. Menton, which has been awarded the first prize in the "Floral Towns" 4 years in succession is now "hors concours 4 flowers".

Surrounding the town are the lovely forest walks with the old villages of Roquebrune, Gorbio, Sainte Agnes *, Castellar and Castillon which look down on the bay and the nearby mountains offer all their splendour e.g. the mountain of Mercantour, the Valley of Merveilles, the forest of Turini, L'Authion and more.

The sun, sea, mountains, colour and perfumes mingle for your delight. Beaches extend in two bays, both with pleasure ports offering all the water sports; regattas, sailing school, water skiing, scuba-diving, boating, big game fishing. Other sports activities include; tennis, swimming pools, golfing (Mont-Angel Golf Course: 18 holes), horse riding, ball trap, petanque etc. Up in the mountains, one can go skiing, climbing, kayak boating and long hikes.

145

With the Casino, restaurants and night clubs, Menton offers a very active social life to please evrybody. Menton has an intense and permanent artistic and cultural activity. Bridge and chess clubs, museum, lectures, concerts and art exhibitions.

The theatrical season is from November to April. The Lemon Festival is held in February. In summertime there is the International Festival of Music in August held in the forecourt of the Old Town's Church of Saint Michel, spectacularly marked by burning flame torches sending away a scent as if to announce that extraordinary events are taking place. The summer season ends with "Musical September".

* Sainte-Agnes, is a small village, 3 km away from the sea and situated at the altitude of 750 m which makes it the highest village in Europe. From Menton it is very well sign-posted.

HOTELS

OF

THE RIVIERA

EUROP HOTEL ★★★

35 Avenue de Verdun,
06500 — Menton
Tel.9335-5992

 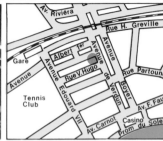

33 rooms with bath or shower, WC ● telephone ● radio ● TV ● min
bar ● lift ● air-conditioned ● sound-proofed ● bar ● garage in th
hotel ● casino and beaches nearby.

HOTEL VICTORIA ★★★

7 Promenade du Cap
06190 — Roquebrune Cap-Martin
Tel.9335-6590

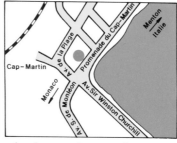

0 rooms with bath, shower and private toilets ● colour TV ●
reakfast only ● many restaurants nearby ● ample parking facilities ●
losed garage for 8 cars ● exceptional view over the Menton Bay and
he approach to Italy.

HOTEL BEAUREGARD ★

10 Rue Albert 1er,
06500 — Menton
Tel.9335-7408

0 rooms with bathroom shower or C de T ● television room ●
estaurant ● attractive garden ● shops,casino and beaches closeby.

HOTEL - RESTAURANT ORLY ★★

27 Porte de France
06500 - Menton
Tel:9335-6081

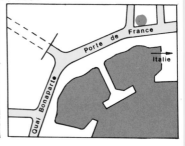

0 rooms with private bathroom ● air-conditioned ● facing the sea
nd beaches ● direct telephone line ● bar ● tee-room ● restaurant
ith terrace ● garage and private parking facilities.

INTER-HOTEL ALEXANDRA ***

93 Avenue Sir Winston Churchill,
06190 Roquebrune Cap-Martin
Tel.9335-6545, Telex:OREM 470673 F 1548

 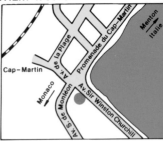

40 rooms with fully equipped bathroom ● air-conditioned ● colour TV
● mini-bar ● direct telephone ● lift ● solarium ● lounge bar ● parking
reserved and garage spaces ● exceptional view over the Menton Bay
and the approach to Italy.

HOTEL WESTMINSTER **

14 Avenue Lois Laurens
Roquebrune Cap-Martin
Tel.9335-0068

 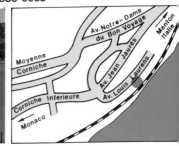

30 rooms with bathroom or shower,WC ● telephone ● TV room ●
attractive garden on a hill with panoramic view on the bay ● bar ●
200 m from the beach.

HOTEL "LE NAPOLEON" **

7 Avenue de la Victoria
06320 — La Turbie
Tel.9341-0054

24 rooms with bathrooms and toilets ● large flowered terrace ● radio
● restaurant ● bar ● telephone ● TV on request ● casino 7 km at
Monaco

ALTEA HOTEL ★★★
Rue du Port
34280 — la Grande-Motte
Tel.6756-9081, Telex: 480241

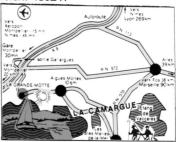

5 rooms ● details page 14 ● restaurant ● bar ● parking ● on the cht harbour in the heart of the well known Languedoc — Roussillon sort area.

ALTEA HOTEL ★★★
Le Polygone, 218 Rue du Bastion — Ventadour,
34000 — Montpellier
Tel.6764-6566, Telex: 480362

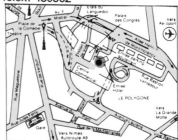

16 rooms ● details page 14 ● restaurant ● bar ● parking ● a modern otel in the heart of Polygone business district 3 min from the Palace e la Comedie.

HOTEL PARIS-NICE ★★
58 Rue de France,
06000 — Nice
Tel.9388-3861

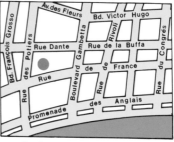

28 rooms equipped with bathrooms and private toilets ● telephone ● TV room ● half-day and full day sight-seeing tours ● half board and full board on request ● car park nearby ● appears to be the nearest 2-star hotel to beaches at Nice and Promenade des Anglais.

PULLMAN HOTEL ***

28 Avenue Notre-Dame,
06000 — Nice
Tel.9380-3024, Telex:470662

 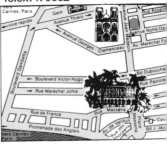

200 rooms ● details, page 14 ● TV with video circuit ● restaurant
bar ● sauna bath ● parking facilities ● 5 min from the Promenade de
Anglais ● tropical garden and swimming pool.

HOTEL DE MULHOUSE **

9 Rue Chauvain,
06000 — Nice
Tel.9392-3669, Telex:970579 TURAZUR

 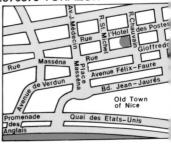

50 rooms with bathroom or shower, WC ● telephone direct
automatic morning call ● cafeteria on 6th floor ● television room ●
200 m from the Massena square

HOTEL "LA BELLE MEUNIERE" *

21 Avenue Durante,
06000 — Nice
Tel.9388-6615

17 rooms with C de T or shower and WC ● elegant and tidy ●
detached, villa-type ● parking facilities ● less than 10 min to the
Promenade des Anglais

PULLMAN BEACH HOTEL **** de Luxe

13 Rue de Canada,
06400 — Cannes
Tel.9338-2232, Telex: 470034

 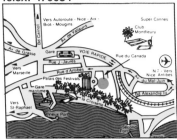

95 rooms ● details, page 14 ● TV with video circuit ● restaurant ● bar ● parking facilities ● open-air swimming pool ● the latest of the luxury hotels ● close to the new Festival and Congress Hall ● 50 m away from the Croisette.

ALTEA HOTEL ****

Boulevard Amiral-Vence,
83200 — Toulon
Tel.9424-4157, Telex:400 347

93 rooms ● details, page 14 ● restaurant ● TV bar ● garden ● parking facilities ● open-air swimming pool ● bowling (French) ● overlooking the famous Toulon roadstead.

PULLMAN ILE ROUSSE **** de Luxe

Boulevard Louis-Lumière,
83150 — Bandol
Tel. 9429-4686, Telex: 400372

 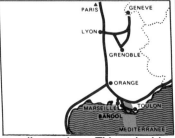

55 de luxe rooms ● bathroom ● radio ● colour TV and video programme ● telephone ● lift ● balcony ● 2 restaurants on the beach ● bar ● 3 conference rooms ● open air swimming pool with sea water ● solarium numerous sport facilities ● garage ● direct access on the beach.

PULLMAN HOTEL BEAUVAU ★★★★
4 Rue Beauvau,
13001 — Marseille
Tel.9154-9100, Telex: 401778

 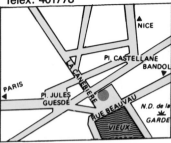

72 rooms with bath or shower ● air-conditioned ● colour TV ● radio ● mini-bar ● lift ● numerous restaurants nearby ● located in the front of the "Vieux Port" near the Canebiere.

ALTEA HOTEL ★★★★
Centre Bourse, Rue Neuve St.Martin
13001 — Marseille
Tel.9191-9129 Telex: 401886

200 rooms ● details page 14 ● TV with video circuit ● restaurant ● bar ● meeting rooms ● located near the old port overlooking the Jardin des Vestipes.

HOTEL CAMARGUE ★★★
Route d'Istres,
13270 — Fos-sur-Mer
Tel.4205-0057, Telex: 410812

 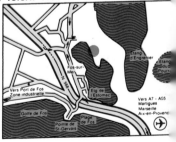

146 rooms ● details page 14 ● restaurant ● bar ● swimming pool ● conference rooms ● parking.

Happiness guaranteed at the Asterix Theme Park!

Just 38 kilometres to the North of Paris, the Asterix Theme Park opens its doors to you from April 4th 1990. Come and spend an unforgettable day in the Park's beautiful surroundings. Meet Asterix and all his friends. You'll find them in the Village of those invincible Gauls, of course, but also at the Roman Camp, packed full of soldiers who get clouted in every way imaginable !

Everywhere you go in Asterix Park, you will chuckle at the antics of Gauls and the Romans. In the arena, be careful not to die laughing during the hilarious cambat between the gladiators and a wily Gaul! Are you daring enough to ride on the biggest roller coaster in Europe, with its heart-stopping 7 loops ? Then race down the Big Splasch, which ends with an 11 metre-long water slide ! At the Lakeside, you can see the fabulous dolphin show.

Then, in the Rue de Paris, you'll travel on a fantastic journey through 1000 years of history, from the Middle Ages to modern times. Explore the lively scenes around you, with the help of craftsmen who recreate the past as you watch. Reconstructions, attractions, all kinds of activities and wonderful shows await you. The Getafix Show offers you a magicians battle using the most sophisticated of special effects. In the 3-D cinema, you will discover anew the wonderful world of nature and animals.

Come soon to spend a magical day at the Asterix Theme Park!

Information:
- Catering facilities: you can find every kind of menu from a quick snack to three-course lunch, with a choice of almost 40 eating places located throughout the Park.
- Services: these include a cloakroom, changing and feeding facilities for babies, pushchair rental, a medical centre, a bureau de change, and a post office.
- Direct access from the A1 highway (exit reserved for Asterix Theme Park)

Enjoy yourself without worrying about how much you spend - the entrance ticket gives you access to all the attractions and shows at the Park.

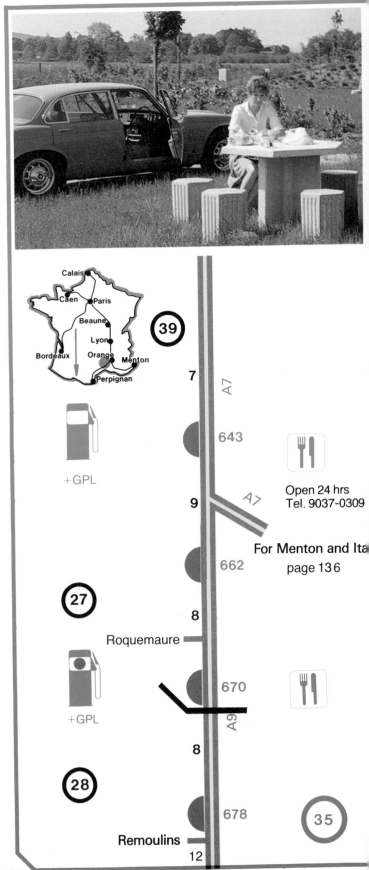

Calais

Caen Paris

Beaune

Lyon

Bordeaux Orange

Menton

Perpignan

39

7

A7

643

Open 24 hrs
Tel. 9037-0309

9   A7

662

For Menton and Ita
page 136

27

8

Roquemaure

+GPL

670

A9

28

8

678

35

Remoulins

12

156

Continued from page 136

Aire de Mornas-Village

This Rest Area's name is shown here for your reference only

Aire de Roquemaure-Ouest

Small with tables and benches.
SOS — at the side of Area.

Aire de Tavel-Nord

Tables and benches among trees and in the open space. Pigue-nique site, forested, apacious and nice. Very well stocked boutique with wide selection of; maps & guide books, foods, fresh fruits, souvenirs, hot & cold drinks from automatic machines.

Aire de Estezargues-Nord

Pique — nique site incorporated, some pretty spots with attractive trees. Spacious, tables and benches.
SOS — at the side of Area. Info-Route.

157

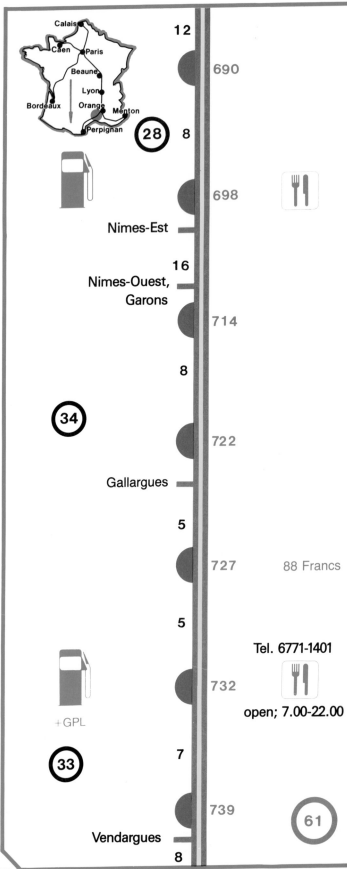

12

690

28   8

698

Nimes-Est

16

Nimes-Ouest,
Garons

714

8

34

722

Gallargues

5

727   88 Francs

5

Tel. 6771-1401

732   open; 7.00-22.00

+GPL

33   7

739   61

Vendargues

8

Aire de Ledenon-Nord

Completely open space type of area, few tables and benches pleasant.
SOS — at the side.

Aire de Nimes-Marguerittes

There is a Pique-mique site with some tables and benches. Open space, pleasant.
SOS — about 500 m past the Rest Area.

Aire de Milhaud-Nord

Small with tables and benches.
SOS — at the side.

Aire de Vergèze-Nord

Pique — nique site, swings, see — saws, sort of a wooden castle for children to play. There are tables and benches.
SOS — at the exit.

Aire de Barrière de péage

Just parking facilities.

Aire de Vidourle

The petrol station boutique offers an exceptional range of car parts and related items, especially in electronics; CB radio specialists - sale and repair. Well stocked in foods, toys, tee-shirts, maps and guides. SOS – at the side of area. Info-Route.

Aire de Nabrigas

There are tables and benches in the open space and among trees, swings and climbing frames.
SOS — at the side of Area.

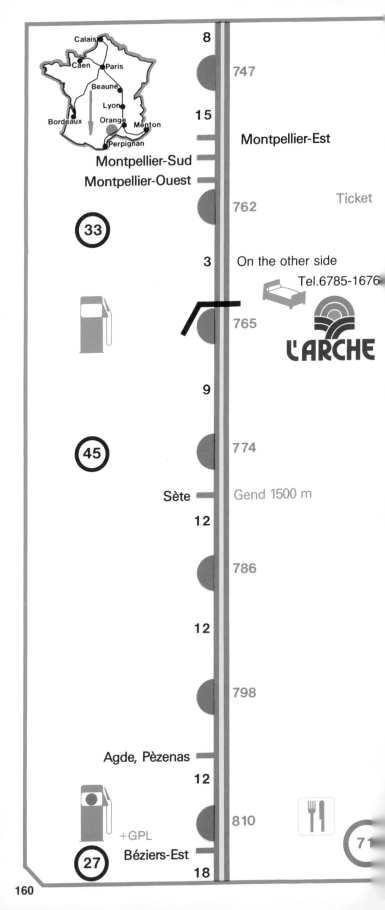

8

747

15

Montpellier-Est

Montpellier-Sud

Montpellier-Ouest

762

Ticket

(33)

3

On the other side

Tel.6785-1676

765

L'ARCHE

9

(45)

774

Sète — Gend 1500 m

12

786

12

798

Agde, Pèzenas

12

+GPL

810

(27)

Béziers-Est

18

71

Aire de St.Aunes-Nord

Tables and benches, small and pretty.
SOS — at the side.

Aire de Barrière de péage

Just parking bay for a few cars.

Aire de Montpellier-Fabregues

Just parking facilities with tables and benches. The petrol station air-conditioned boutique offers wide range of; car parts, toys, maps and guide books, foods and drinks, pottery, tee-shirts, exceptional selection of toiletry and perfumes. SOS at the exit.

Aire de Gigean

Open space type of area, yet with some trees. There are tables and benches.
SOS — at the side.

Aire de Meze

Forested with a pique — nique site incorporated. There are tables and benches.
SOS – 500 m past the area.

Aire de Florensac

Just parking spaces.
SOS — at the side of Area.

Aire de Béziers-Montblanc

Generally, car parking facilities. Info-Route.
SOS — at the side.

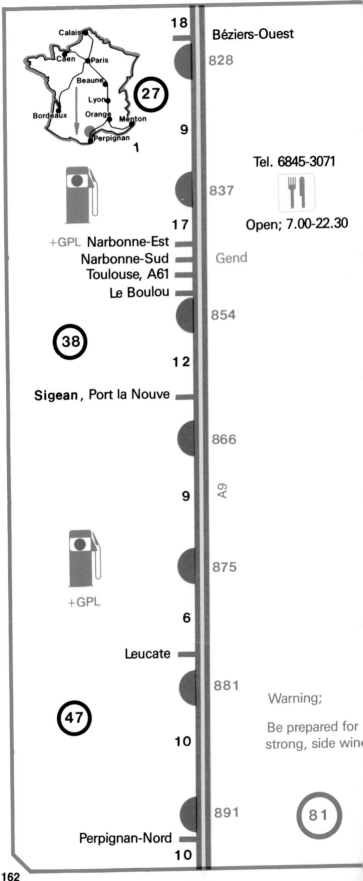

Béziers-Ouest

828

18

9

837

27

1

Tel. 6845-3071

Open; 7.00-22.30

+GPL **Narbonne-Est**
Narbonne-Sud
Toulouse, A61
Le Boulou

17

Gend

854

38

12

Sigean, Port la Nouve

866

9

A9

875

+GPL

6

Leucate

881

47

10

Warning;

Be prepared for
strong, side wind

891

81

Perpignan-Nord

10

162

Aire de Lespignan

Open space, with tables and benches. Small and pleasant.
SOS — at the side of Rest Area.

Aire de Narbonne-Vinassan

Pique — nique jeux d'enfants, tables and benches. modest
in size. Cafeteria, resstaurant, self — service.
SOS — at the side. Info-Route.

Aire de Prat de Cest

Slightly forested,on a raised ground. Tables and benches.
Incorporates a picnic site.
SOS — at the entry to the Area.

Aire des Gasparets

Tables and benches among trees, combinated with a
picnic site.
SOS — at the side of Area.

Aire de Lapalme

Some tables and benches.
SOS — at the side. Info-Route.

Aire de Fitou-Ouest

Very much, open type area, lit at night,just few benches.
SOS — at the side of the Rest Area.

Aire de Chateau de Salses

Tables and benches, open type with bushy trees. Tunnel
to the other side of Motorway Services. Very nice.

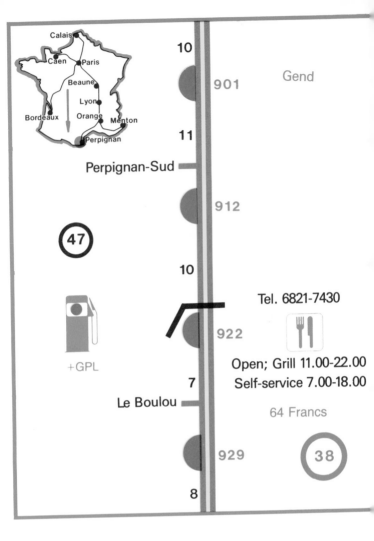

10

901

Gend

11

Perpignan-Sud

912

47

10

Tel. 6821-7430

922

Open; Grill 11.00-22.00
Self-service 7.00-18.00

7

Le Boulou

64 Francs

929

38

8

+GPL

SPAIN

ALTEA HOTEL ✱✱✱
26 Rue de Coubertin,
71000 — Macon
Tel.8536-2806, Telex:800830

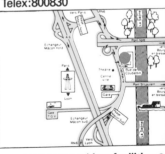

63 room ● details, page 14 ● restaurant ● bar ● parking facilities ●
garden ● boutique ● 100 m away from in-door and open-air
swimming pool ● on the bank of Saone River ● surrounded by green
country side.

Aire de **Rivesaltes**

Grassy, attractive trees, pleasantly arranged site. Very pretty.
SOS — located at the entry.

Aire Ouest de **Pavillons**

Open type, lit at night. Tables and benches, pretty.
SOS — at the entry.

Aire du **Village Catalon**

Very spacious, away from the Petrol Station Complex. Well sign — posted. Unusually big picnicking area with shops nearby. Info-Route.

Aire de **Barrière de péage**

Just parking bay.

ALTEA HOTEL ★★★★
7 Rue Labeda
31000 — Toulouse
Tel.6121-2175, Telex: 530550

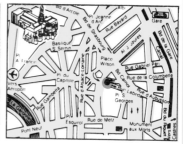

95 rooms ● details page 14 ● radio ● TV ● direct telephone ●
mini-bar ● restaurant ● bar ● parking.

Since beginning our service between Ramsgate and Dunkerque in 1981, we have gained a reputation amongst discerning travellers for quality and comfort.

THE FINEST FOOD

On board, you can enjoy the finest food across the Channel.... a sumptuous breakfast buffet on the first morning sailings and our famous Scandinavian Smorgasbord and hot carvery during the rest of the day.

FUN FOR YOU AND THE CHILDREN

There's a choice of comfortable bars to relax in and a play area for the tots. For your further entertaiment you'll find video games for children of all ages, as well as British television programmes to watch.

DUTY-FREE SHOPPING

A visit to our duty-free shops is a wonderful opportunity to indulge yourself - and save money, too. You'll be spoiled for choice, selecting bargains galore from our superb range of duty-free goods.

MOST CONVENIENT ROUTE TO EUROPE

Ramsgate is no further from London than Dover and quickly reached via the M2. And Dunkerque is easily the most convenient French Port for the British motorist. It's situated right at the start of the Franch motorway system giving you quick access to Belgium, Germany and Austria, as well as France.

BOOKING IS EASY

You have a choice of five sailings a day in each direction so planning your journey is simple. Book with Sally and discover the best kept secret in cross Channel travel. For further details just drop into your local Travel Agent or call our Ferry Reservation office on

Ramsgate (0843) 595522

WE ♥ LEAD-FREE

The actual Routes of the Guide

(going north)

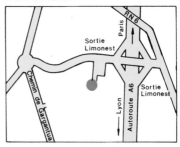

Aire de Pia

 Gend

Few tables and benches, some trees. Lit at night. Nice
SOS — at the side of Area.

Aire Est des Pavillons

Forested, few benches, very pleasant.
SOS — at the side.

Aire du Village Catalon

Very spacious area with picnicking facilities away from pet
station complex. Sign-posted. Info-Route.

Aire de Barrière de péage

Just parking bay for cars.

HOTEL LA COUCHEE **

Aire de Port – Lauragais, Autoroute A61,
31290 Avignonet - Lauragais.
Tel.6127-1712, Telex:531281

42 rooms with bathrooms ● colour TV ● direct telphone ● automatic
morning call ● parking ● open-air swimming pool ● tennis ●
restaurant "La Dinée" - cuisine régionale ● rooms for disabled
people ● conference rooms.

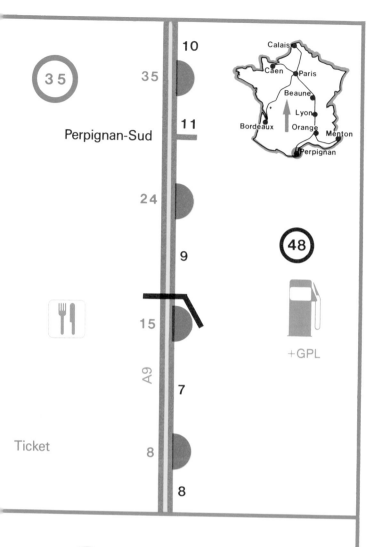

35

Perpignan-Sud

10

35

11

Calais
Caen
Paris
Beaune
Lyon
Bordeaux
Orange
Menton
Perpignan

24

9

48

+GPL

15

A9

7

Ticket

8

8

SPAIN

Aire de Lespignan

Tables and benches, lit at night, some trees.
SOS — at side.

Aire de Narbonne-Vinnassan

Pique — nique jeux d'enfants, located on a raised ground.
Tables and benches, a lot of trees, very
large. Recommended.

Aire de Bages

Grassy, tables and benches, lit at night. Very spacious and
pretty.
SOS — by the exit of the Area.

Aire de Sigean

A picnic area incorporated also, tables and benches among
trees. Lit at night. Very nice.
SOS — at the side.

Aire de Lapalme

Open space type of area, yet with some trees. Tables and
benches.
SOS — at side.

Aire de Fitou-Est

Open space type of area, some trees, spacious.
SOS — at the side.

Aire de Château de Salses

Forested, connected with the other side of Motorway's
Rest Area serwices by a tunnel.
SOS — at the side.

Béziers-Ouest

74

109

18

27

9 --

100

17

Narbonne-Est
Narbonne-Sud
Toulouse, A61

83

See page 168

Sigean

12

71

37

MONTAUBAN
Pont de Chaume - Rocade Est -
82000 Montauban
Tél. 63.20.20.88

A9

8

63

9

Leucate

Warning;

Be prepared for
strong side winds

54

9

48

45

Perpignan-Nord

10

+GPL

HOTEL
ARCADE

Aire de Saint Aunes-Sud

Stone made tables and benches, few trees. Small and pretty.
SOS — at side.

Aire de Barrière de péage

Just parking spaces.

Aire de Montpellier-Fabreques

Very spacious, forested, mainly parking spaces. Footbridge to the other side of motorway Rest Area. Info-Route.

Aire de Gigean

Lit at night, mainly car spaces, few tables and benches.
SOS — at side.

Aire de Loupian

Open space type of area with some trees and picnic area.
Lit at night, tables and benches. Spacious.
SOS — at the entry.

Aire de Florensac

Just parking spaces, but pleasant.
SOS — close to the entry.

Aire de Béziers-Montblanc

Very spacious in parking facilities, some benches.
SOS — close to the entry.

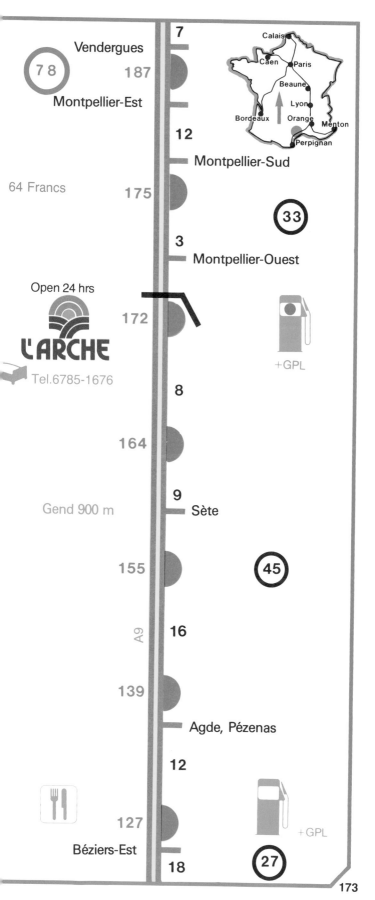

Vendergues

7 8

187

Montpellier-Est

64 Francs

175

7

12

Montpellier-Sud

33

3

Montpellier-Ouest

Open 24 hrs

L'ARCHE

Tel.6785-1676

172

8

164

9 Sète

Gend 900 m

155

45

A9 16

139

Agde, Pézenas

12

127

Béziers-Est

18

27

173

Aire de Ledenon-Sud

Open space type, stone made tables and benches, small.
Nice.
SOS — at side.

Aire de Nimes-Marguerittes

Ample parking facilities, cafeteria, grill,boutique.
SOS — at the exit. Info-Route.

Aire de Milhaud-Sud

Small with few tables and benches.
SOS — by the exit.

Aire de Vergeze-Sud

Forested, picnic area with a lot of tables and benches.
SOS — actually on the Rest area.

Aire de Barrière de péage

Seems to offer no facilities of any kind.

Aire de Vidourle

Mainly car parking spaces. Cafeteria.
SOS — at side.

Aire de Mas du Roux

Pique-nique jeux d'enfants,tables and benches among tree
and in the open. Very pretty and recommended.
SOS — at side.

59

🍴

Ticket

🍴

11

246

8

238

15

Nimes-Est

Nimes-Ouest, Marseille

223

9

214

4

210

Gallargues

5

205

11

194

7

Marseille

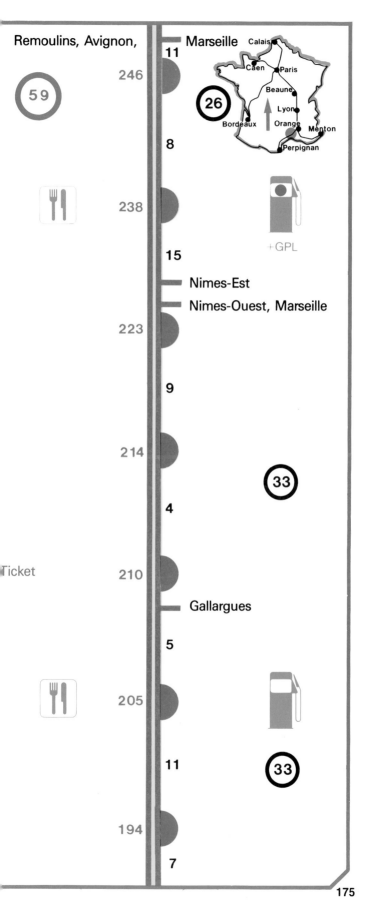

26

+GPL

33

33

HOTEL MERCURE ✱✱✱

Autoroute A7
13680 — Lancon-de-Provence
Tel. 9042-8711, Telex:440183 F

 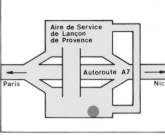

100 rooms (including 1 for disabled people and 2 suites) with fully equipped bathrooms ● colour TV (partly) ● direct line telephone ● mini-bar ● air-conditioning ● sound proofing ● catering from 7 p.m. to midnight ● swimming pool ● buffet brekfast ● bar-open until midnight ● free car park.

Aire de Mormas

This Rest Area's name is shown here for your reference only

To continue for Porte de Lyon and Paris turn over to pag 184.

Aire de Roquemaure-Est

Open space area, yet with tables and benches among trees. Small and pretty.
SOS — at the exit.

Aire de Tavel-Sud

Incorporated a picnic area facilities. Restaurant, bar and boutique. Info-Route.

Aire de Estezergues-Sud

Very spacious with some bushy trees, tables and benches.
SOS — at side.

HOTEL MERCURE ✱ ✱ ✱

Autoroute A6 71260 Saint - Albain - Lugny
Tel:8533-1900, Telex:800 881

100 luxurious rooms with fully equipped bathroom ● fully sound proofed ● air-conditioned ● direct telephone lines ● mini-bar ● colour TV ● open-air swimming pool ● terrace.

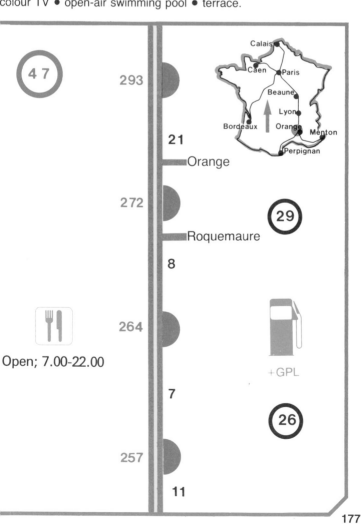

4 7

293

21

Orange

272

29

Roquemaure

8

Open; 7.00-22.00

264

+GPL

7

26

257

11

Aire des Bréguières

Very spacious which is not apparent at first. Tables and benches, nice area. There is a Musee de L'Automobiliste.
SOS — 200 m before entry. Info-Route

Aire de Barrière de péage

As below.

Aire de Barrière de péage

As below.

Aire de Barrière de péage

Small with parking facilities.
SOS — 400 metres past the area.

Aire de la Scoperta

Open space type of area but with a lot of small trees. Tables and benches, very elegant place. Bar, buffet.
SOS — at the side.

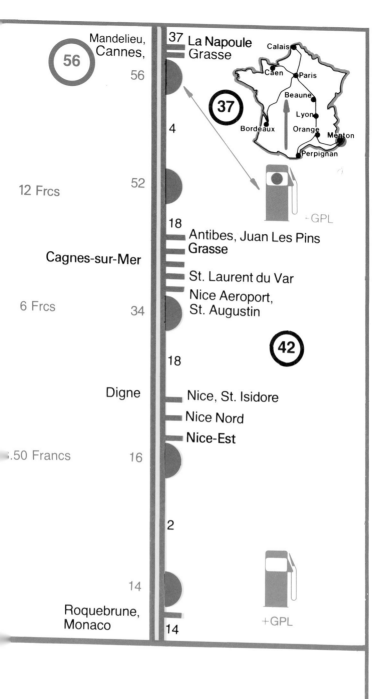

56 Mandelieu,
Cannes,
56

37 La Napoule
Grasse

Calais
Caen Paris
Beaune
37 Lyon
Bordeaux Orange Menton
Perpignan

- GPL

4

52

12 Frcs

18

Antibes, Juan Les Pins
Grasse

Cagnes-sur-Mer

St. Laurent du Var

Nice Aeroport,
St. Augustin

6 Frcs 34

42

18

Digne

Nice, St. Isidore

Nice Nord

Nice-Est

.50 Francs 16

2

14

Roquebrune,
Monaco

+GPL

14

MENTON

Aire de Rousset

Very open, just car parking spaces. Bar, cafeteria.
SOS — at the side.

Aire de St. Hilaire

Open type of area with some trees. There are tables and benches.
SOS — by the entry.

Aire Nord de Cambarette

Open space type, few tables and benches. Restaurant, bar.
SOS — at the side. Info-Route.

Aire de Candumy

Forested, tables and benches, rather large area sited on a hill. Nice.
SOS — by the entry.

Aire de Vidauban-Nord

Just parking facilities.
SOS — by the exit.

Aire du Canaver

Spacious area, tables and benches, some trees. Very nice.
Bar — restaurant. SOS - past the area.

Aire de Barrière de péage

Small, couple of sets of tables and benches.
SOS — close to the entry.

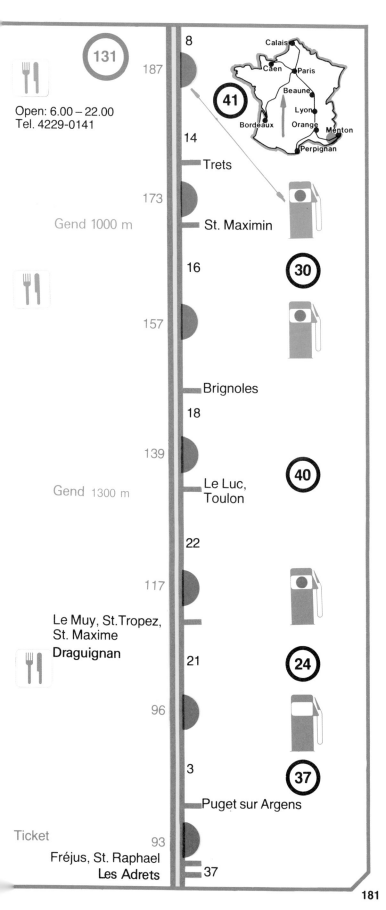

(131)

Open: 6.00 – 22.00
Tel. 4229-0141

Gend 1000 m

8
187

14
Trets

173
St. Maximin

16
(30)

157

Brignoles

18

139
(40)

Gend 1300 m
Le Luc,
Toulon

22

117

Le Muy, St.Tropez,
St. Maxime
Draguignan

21
(24)

96

3
(37)

Puget sur Argens

Ticket
93
Fréjus, St. Raphael
Les Adrets

37

41

Calais
Caen
Paris
Beaune
Lyon
Bordeaux
Orange
Menton
Perpignan

Aire de Sénas

No tables, just benches. Very small, tidy and interesting.
SOS — by the entry.

Aire de Lamanon

Forested, jungle like type, spacious, plenty of tables and benches. Pique-nique jeux d'enfants.
SOS — 300 m before entry.

Aire de Barrière de péage

In a stage of development.

Aire de Lançon de Provence

It is an open type of area, yet with tables and benches among trees. Very pleasant. Footbridge to the other side of the motorway.
SOS — at the side. Info-Route.

Aire de Ventabren-Nord

Open type of area with some shady spots. Pique-nique jeux d'enfants. Recommended. SOS – 400 m past the area.

Aire de Barrière de péage

Very small. Gendarmerie Station.

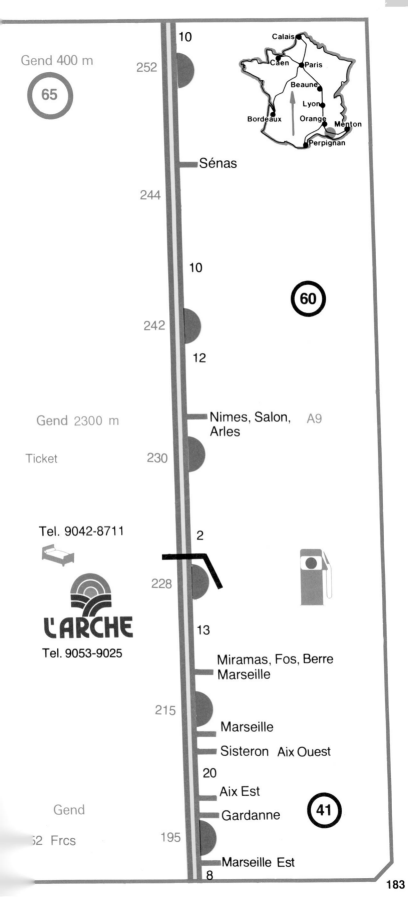

Gend 400 m

65

252
10

Sénas

244

10

60

242

12

Nimes, Salon, A9
Arles

Gend 2300 m

Ticket

230

Tel. 9042-8711

2

228

L'ARCHE

Tel. 9053-9025

13

Miramas, Fos, Berre
Marseille

215

Marseille

Sisteron Aix Ouest

20

Aix Est

Gend

Gardanne **41**

195

2 Frcs

Marseille Est

8

Aire de Donzère

Completely open type of area, with tables and benches, very elegant. Small.
SOS — at the side.

Aire de Tricastin

Very small and elegant place with tables and benches.
Recommended. SOS – 400 m past the area.

Aire de Mornas

Spacious, just parking facilities.
SOS — at the side. Info-Route.

Aire d' Orange-Le Coudolet

Pique-nique jeux d'enfants. Large and elegant.
SOS – 200 m past the area.

Aire de Sorgues

Pique-nique jeux d'enfants. Spacious and nice.
Restaurant, bar, boutique.
SOS — at the side. Info-Route.

Aire de Noves

Open type with tables and benches, very elegant.
SOS — by the entry.

Aire de Cavaillon

Open type of area, sited on a hill by a water reservoir, sort of a lake. Small and nice. SOS – 300 m before the entry.

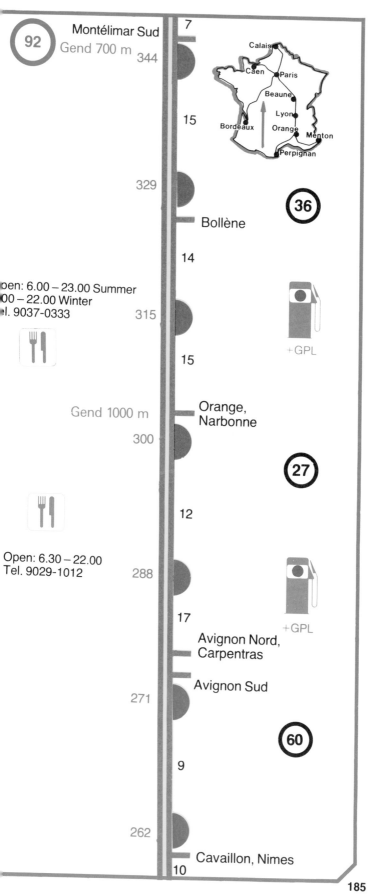

92

Montélimar Sud
Gend 700 m   344

7

15

329

Bollène

14

Open: 6.00 – 23.00 Summer
.00 – 22.00 Winter
el. 9037-0333

315

15

36

+GPL

Gend 1000 m

Orange,
Narbonne

300

27

12

Open: 6.30 – 22.00
Tel. 9029-1012

288

17

Avignon Nord,
Carpentras

+GPL

Avignon Sud

271

60

9

262

Cavaillon, Nimes

10

Aire de Latitude 45

Very open, yet some trees. Tables and benches. Very nice.
SOS — at the side.

Aire de Portes-Lès-Valence

Pique-nique jeux d'enfants, small and open type of area.
SOS - at the side of area. Info-Route.

Aire de Livron

Very small with some tables and benches.
SOS — at side.

Aire de Saulce

Pique-nique jeux d'enfants. Very small but pretty and recommended.
SOS — just past the exit.

Aire du Logis Neuf

Pique-nique jeux d'enfants. Large, very nice. Recommended.
SOS — by the entry.

Aire du Roubion

Pique-nique jeux d'enfants. Very small, open type and nice.
SOS — at the entry.

Aire de Montélimar

Pique-nique jeux d'enfants. Large with nests of tables and benches in the open and among trees. Nice.
SOS — at the side. Info-Route.

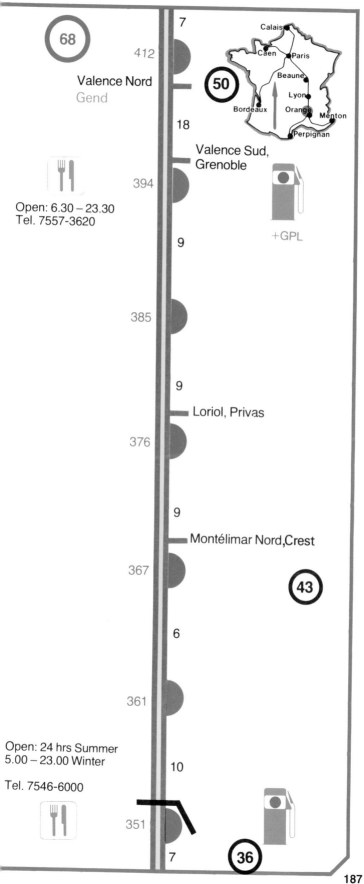

68

7

412

Valence Nord
Gend

50

18

Valence Sud,
Grenoble

394

+GPL

9

385

9

Loriol, Privas

376

9

Montélimar Nord, Crest

367

43

6

361

10

Calais
Caen
Paris
Beaune
Lyon
Bordeaux
Orange
Menton
Perpignan

Open: 6.30 – 23.30
Tel. 7557-3620

Open: 24 hrs Summer
5.00 – 23.00 Winter

Tel. 7546-6000

351

7

36

Aire de Barrière de péage

Very small and limited.

Aire de la Grande Borne

Pique-nique jeux d'enfants. Plenty of nests of tables and stools. Very nice. Recommended.
SOS - by the entry.

Aire de St. Rambert d'Albon

Pique-nique jeux d'enfants. Recommended.
SOS - at the side. Info-Route.

Aire de la Combe Tourmente

Pique-nique jeux d'enfants. Recommended.
SOS — at the side.

Aire de la Galaure

Pique-nique jeux d'enfants. Nests of tables and benches among trees. Nice.
SOS – at the exit.

Aire de la Bouterne

Open type of area, tables and benches, very small.
SOS — at the end of the area, by the exit.

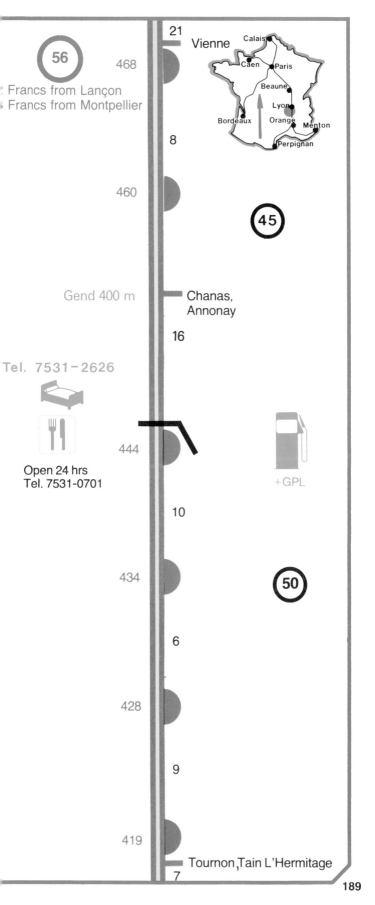

56

468

Francs from Lançon
Francs from Montpellier

21

Vienne

Calais
Caen Paris
Beaune
Lyon
Bordeaux Orange Menton
Perpignan

45

8

460

Gend 400 m

Chanas,
Annonay

16

Tel. 7531-2626

Open 24 hrs
Tel. 7531-0701

444

+GPL

10

434

50

6

428

9

419

Tournon, Tain L'Hermitage

7

189

Aire de Taponas

Tables and benches.
SOS — at the side.

Aire de Boitray

Newly built 1986. Very spacious, by the water reservoir.
Tables and benches. Lit at night. Very attractive. Coffee
bar. Recommended. SOS – at the side.

Aire de Barrière de péage

Small and pleasant.

Aire de Chères

There are tables and benches. Spacious
SOS — at the side by the exit.

Aire de Paisy

As below.

Aire de Piérre Benite

There are tables and benches.

Aire de Sérézin sur Rhône

Just parking facilities. Grill and sandwich bar.

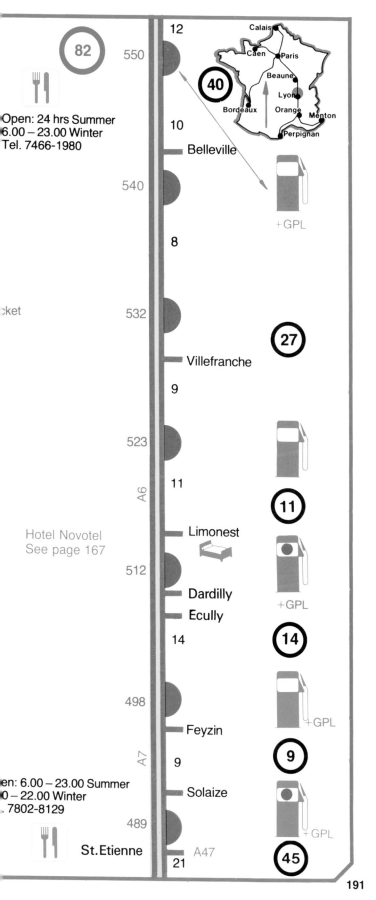

82

🍴

Open: 24 hrs Summer
6.00 – 23.00 Winter
Tel. 7466-1980

cket

Hotel Novotel
See page 167

en: 6.00 – 23.00 Summer
0 – 22.00 Winter
. 7802-8129

🍴

St.Etienne

12

550

40

10

Belleville

540

+GPL

8

532

27

Villefranche

9

523

11

A6

11

Limonest

512

+GPL

Dardilly

Ecully

14

14

498

+GPL

Feyzin

A7

9

9

Solaize

489

+GPL

A47

21

45

Calais
Caen · Paris
Beaune
Lyon
Bordeaux · Orange
Menton
Perpignan

Aire de la Loyère

There are tables and benches, very small but smart enough to be recommended.
SOS — at the side.

Aire de St. Ambreuil

Just parking spaces. Restaurant, bar.
SOS – at the side.

Aire de Boyer

Very small and grassy.
SOS — at the side.

Aire d' Uchizy

Very small and nice. Tables and benches.
SOS — at the side.

Aire de Mâcon-la-Salle

Just parking spaces
SOS — by the exit.

Aire de la Grisière

Very few tables and benches, small but nice.
SOS — at the side of the Area.

Aire de Sablons

It is very unusual in its form, newly built, interesting origination. Recommended.
SOS — at the side.

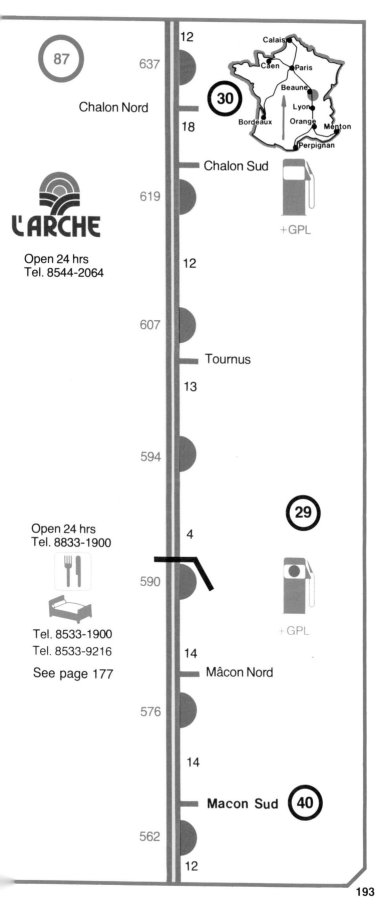

87

Chalon Nord

L'ARCHE

Open 24 hrs
Tel. 8544-2064

30

637

12

18

Chalon Sud

+GPL

619

12

607

Tournus

13

594

Open 24 hrs
Tel. 8833-1900

29

4

590

+GPL

Tel. 8533-1900
Tel. 8533-9216

See page 177

14

Mâcon Nord

576

14

Macon Sud 40

562

12

Calais
Caen Paris
Beaune
Lyon
Bordeaux Orange
Menton
Perpignan

Aire de **Marcigny**

Forested, tables and benches, pretty.
SOS — at the side by the exit.

Aire des **Lochères**

Small, few tables and benches.
SOS — just past the exit.

Aire de **Rèpotte**

Small and nice, tables and benches.
SOS — by the entry.

Aire du **Creux Moreau**

Elegant place with some tables and benches.
SOS — at the side.

Aire du **Bois des Corbeaux**

In two parts; forested and open space, tables and benches, nice.
SOS — at the side.

Aire de **Savigny les Beaune**

Very open type, tables and benches, nice place.
SOS — at the side.

Aire de **Beaune-Merceuil**

Ample parking area in every way.
SOS — at the side.

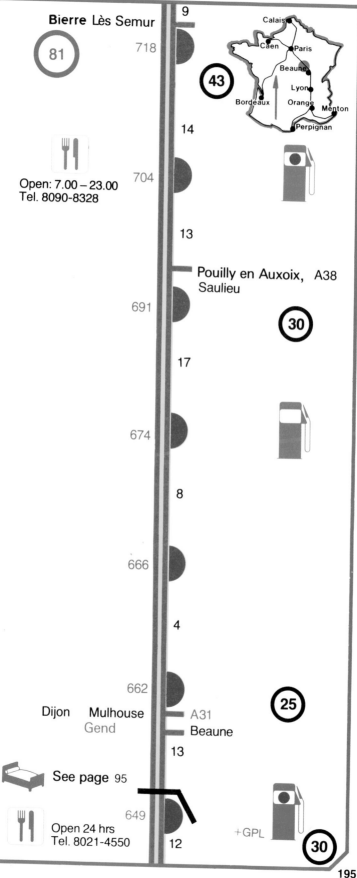

Bierre Lès Semur

81

Open: 7.00 – 23.00
Tel. 8090-8328

9

718

14

704

13

Pouilly en Auxoix, A38
Saulieu

43

30

691

17

674

8

666

4

662

Dijon   Mulhouse   A31
        Gend   Beaune

25

13

See page 95

Open 24 hrs
Tel. 8021-4550

649

12

+GPL

30

Aire de Venoy Soleil Levant

Just parking spaces. A footbridge to the other side of motorway. Info-Route.

Aire du Buisson Rond

Again, as below, very nice.
SOS — by the entry.

Aire du Chevreuil

Again, jungle like type, recommended.
SOS — at the side.

Aire d' Hervaux

Very nice, jungle like type of area, spacious with tables and benches.
SOS — at the side.

Aire de Maison-Dieu

Just parking spaces.
SOS — at the side.

Aire de Genetoy

No tables or benches, completely open.
SOS – at the side towards the entry.

Aire de Côme

Just one lane parking area with no other services provided.
SOS — at the exit.

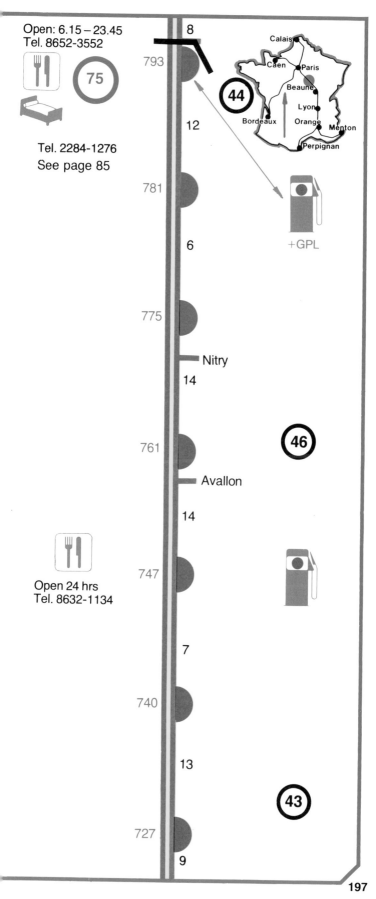

Open: 6.15 – 23.45
Tel. 8652-3552

🍴 75

🛏

Tel. 2284-1276
See page 85

8

793

12

781

6

775

Nitry

14

Avallon

14

747

7

🍴

Open 24 hrs
Tel. 8632-1134

740

13

727

9

44

46

+GPL

43

Calais
Caen Paris
Beaune
Lyon
Bordeaux Orange
Menton
Perpignan

761

Aire d' Egreville

Open space type of area, partly forested. There are tables and benches.
SOS – at the side of area.

Aire de la Roche

As below.
SOS – at the side of area.

Aire des Chènes

Forested area with tables and benches.
SOS – at the side of area.

Aire de la Couline

Basically, just parking spaces.
SOS – at the side.

Aire de la Loupière

Tables and benches among trees.
SOS – at the side of area.

Aire des Pâtures

Partly open area, partly forested. Tables and benches.
SOS — by the entry.

Aire du Thureau

Tables and benches among trees. See-saws, swings, rocking things.
SOS — at the side.

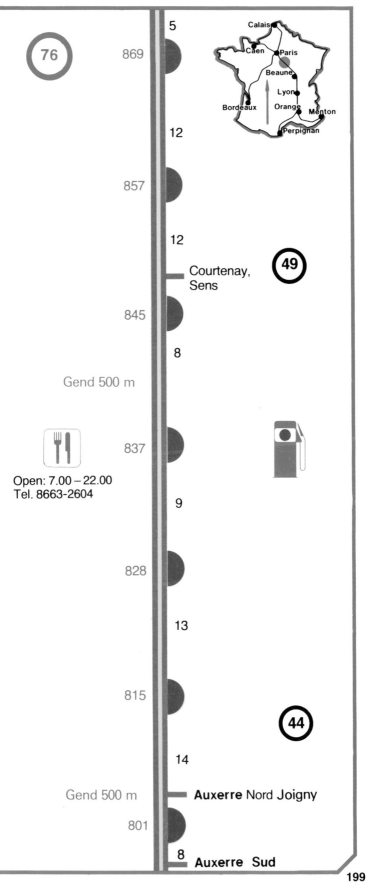

76

869 5

857 12

12

Courtenay,
Sens

49

845

8

Gend 500 m

Open: 7.00 – 22.00
Tel. 8663-2604

837

9

828

13

815

44

14

Gend 500 m   **Auxerre** Nord Joigny

801

8   **Auxerre Sud**

Aire de Villabè

Just spaces for parking.
SOS — at the side.

Aire de St. Sauveur

SOS at the side of the parking area.

Aire de Barrière de péage

Just parking spaces. Gendarmerie Station.

Aire d' Arbonne

Few tables and benches among trees.
SOS — at the side of the Area.

Aire d' Achères

Small and simple.
SOS — at the side.

Aire de Darvault (Nemours)

Ample range of quality services. Interconnected with the
other side Rest Area. SOS – on the rest area.

Aire de Floée

Small, few tables and benches.
SOS — at the side.

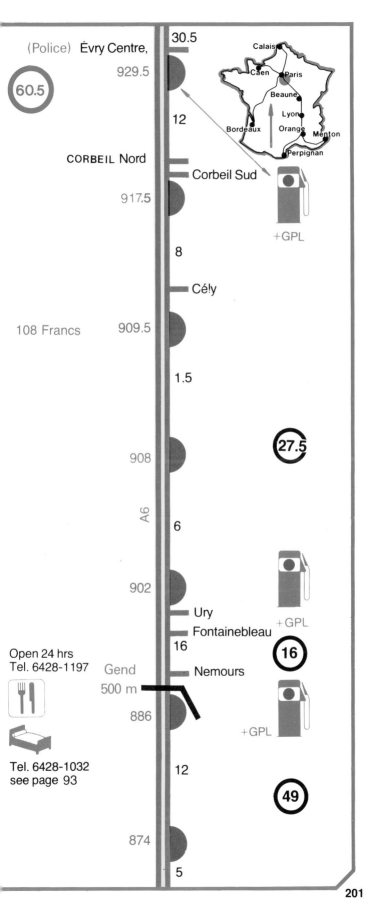

(Police) Évry Centre,

60.5

929.5

30.5

12

CORBEIL Nord

Corbeil Sud

917.5

+GPL

8

Cély

108 Francs

909.5

1.5

27.5

908

A6

6

902

Ury

+GPL

Fontainebleau

Open 24 hrs
Tel. 6428-1197

16

16

Gend
500 m

Nemours

Tel. 6428-1032
see page 93

886

+GPL

12

49

874

5

201

Aire de Roberval-Est

Open space type of area, tables and benches, very nice.
SOS — by the entry.

Aire de Barrière de péage

Spacious.

Aire de Vemars

Just parking spaces provided.

Aire de Villeron

Sited on the side of a hill, tables and benches. Grassy area.
Nice. SOS – 300 m past the area.

Petrol Station Services

Just parking spaces.

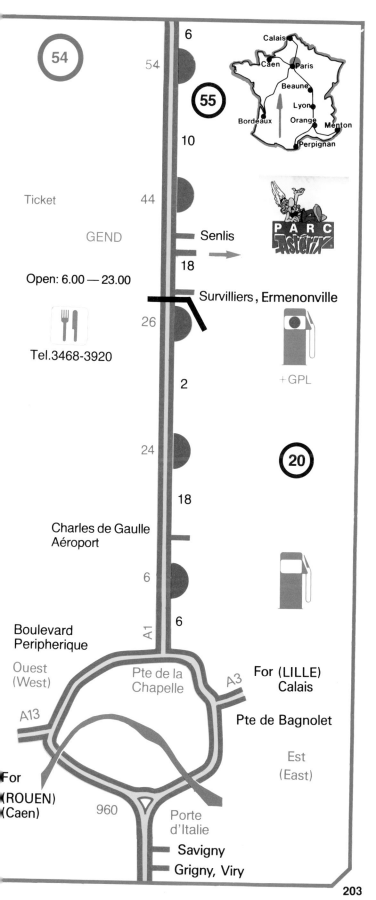

54

55

6

54

10

Ticket

44

GEND

Senlis

18

Open: 6.00 — 23.00

Survilliers, Ermenonville

26

Tel.3468-3920

+ GPL

2

24

20

18

Charles de Gaulle
Aéroport

6

6

Boulevard
Peripherique

A1

Ouest
(West)

Pte de la
Chapelle

A3

For (LILLE)
Calais

A13

Pte de Bagnolet

For
(ROUEN)
(Caen)

960

Est
(East)

Porte
d'Italie

Savigny

Grigny, Viry

Calais
Caen   Paris
Beaune
Lyon
Bordeaux   Orange   Menton
Perpignan

Aire d' Assevillers

Just parking facilities, grassy area. There are; boutique, cafeteria, self-service.
SOS — at the entry.

Aire de Fonches

Open space type of area with tables and benches. Nice.
SOS — at the side.

Aire de Goyencourt-Est

Small, tidy and very nice.
SOS — at the side.

Aire de Tilloloy-Est

Plenty of tables and benches among trees. Nice.
SOS — at the side

Aire de Ressons-Est

Just spaces for parking. Very pleasant. Bar buffet.
SOS — by the entry.

Aire de Remy

Generally open space type of area but there are lots of tables and benches among trees. Very nice. Lit.
SOS - by the entry.

Aire de Chevrières

Lot of trees, tables and benches, spacious and nice.
SOS — 200 m past the area.

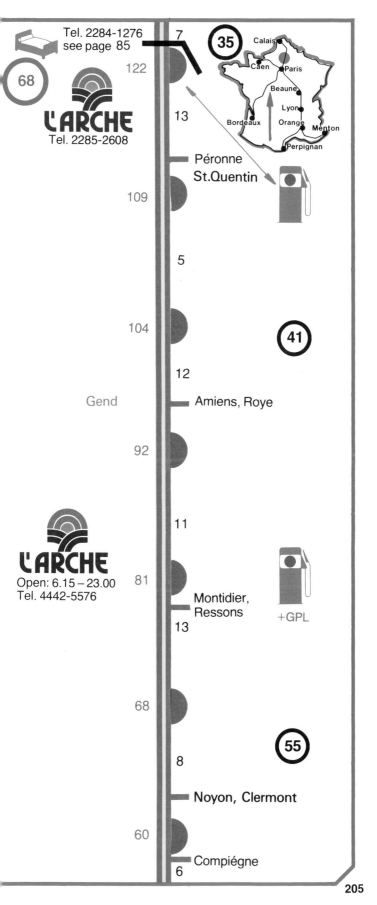

Tel. 2284-1276
see page 85

68

L'ARCHE
Tel. 2285-2608

7

35

122

13

Péronne
St.Quentin

109

5

104

41

12

Gend

Amiens, Roye

92

11

L'ARCHE
Open: 6.15 – 23.00
Tel. 4442-5576

81

Montidier,
Ressons

+GPL

13

68

55

8

Noyon, Clermont

60

Compiégne

6

Aire de la Grande Bucaille

Tables and benches in the open and among trees, small.
Recommended.
SOS — at the side.

Aire d' Angres

Spacious, grassy, no tables nor benches.
SOS — at the side.

Aire de la Cressonniere

Open space type, nice
SOS – at the side by the entry.

Aire de Wancourt-Est

It is partly newly-built, open space type of area and very
attractive.
SOS — at the side.

Aire de Croisilles

Few tables and benches.
SOS — at the side.

Aire de Beaulencourt

As below.
SOS — at the side.

Aire de Feuilleres

Small, grassy with tables and benches.
SOS — at the side.

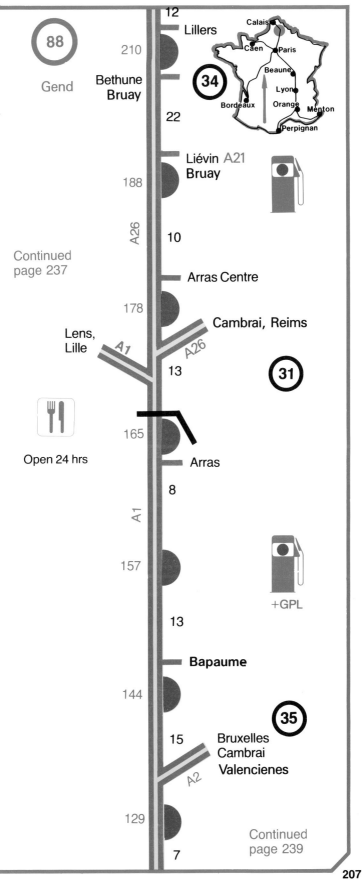

88

Gend

Lillers

210

Bethune
Bruay

22

Liévin A21
Bruay

188

A26

10

Continued
page 237

Arras Centre

178

Cambrai, Reims

Lens,
Lille

A1   A26

13

31

Open 24 hrs

165

Arras

8

A1

157

+GPL

13

Bapaume

144

35

15

Bruxelles
Cambrai
Valencienes

A2

129

Continued
page 239

7

12

34

Calais
Caen Paris
Beaune
Lyon
Bordeaux Orange Menton
Perpignan

207

HOTEL "LE RELAIS" **

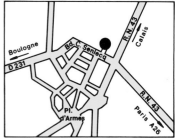

PORT

Aire de Nortkerque

Newly built, very elegant.
SOS - actually on the rest area.

Aire de Barrière de péage

Just parking spaces. Gendarmerie Station.

Aire de Villefleur

Open space type, small with tables and benches. Nice.
SOS — at the side.

Aire de St. Hilaire Cottes

Spacious and grassy.
SOS — at the side.

CALAIS

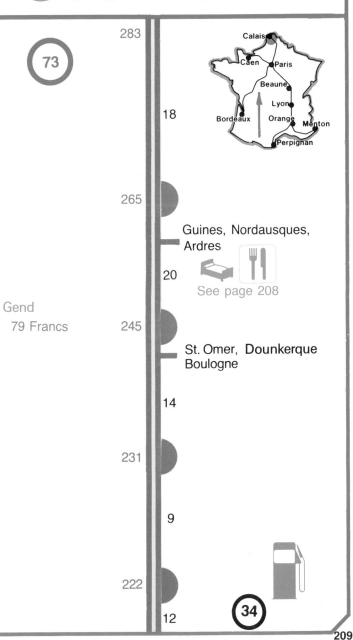

283

73

18

265

Guines, Nordausques,
Ardres

See page 208

20

Gend
79 Francs

245

St. Omer, Dounkerque
Boulogne

14

231

9

222

12

34

Aire de Boisredon

Open type of Area, tables and benches. Swings, very pleasant. Recommended.
SOS — at the side of Area.

Aire de Saugon

Tables and benches, very spacious Area. Very nice indeed. Recommended.
SOS — at the side. Info-Route.

Aire de Cézac

Forested, lit at night. Suitable for picnicking, with tables and benches, spacious. Very nice. Recommended.
SOS — at the side.

Aire de Barrière de péage

Small, few benches, no tables. Very pleasant Area.

Petrol Station Services

Well stocked shop with full range of goods.
SOS — 200 m past the Station Area.

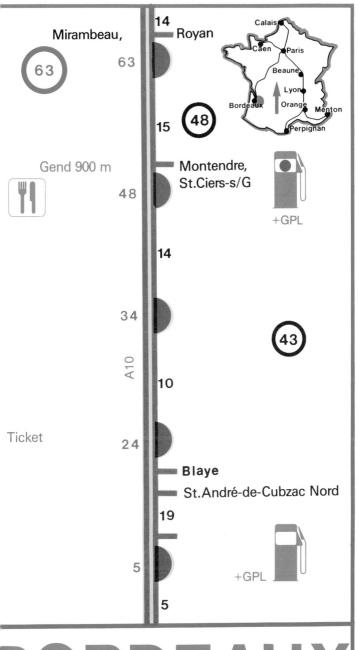

Mirambeau,

63

14 — Royan

63

48

15

Gend 900 m

Montendre,
St.Ciers-s/G

48

+GPL

14

34

43

A10

10

Ticket

24

Blaye
St.André-de-Cubzac Nord

19

5

+GPL

5

BORDEAUX

Aire de la Benâte

Bigger than average in size. Tables and benches in the open and among trees, swings, rocking things. Lit at night. Very nice.
SOS — at the entry.

Aire de Fenioux

Open type of area, located just past the petrol station. Climbing frames, swings.
SOS — at the side. Info-Route.

Aire de Port d'Envaux

Tables and benches in the open and among trees. Climbing things, swings, small and pretty. Recommended.
SOS — by the entry.

Aire de Chermignac

Tables and benches, swings, small trees, bushes. Pretty and attractive enough to be recommended.
SOS — at the side.

Aire de Saint-Léger

Tables and benches. Interconnected by a Tunnel. Very nice. Slides, swings, see-saws. Strongly recommended.
SOS — at the exit of Area. Info-Route.

Aire de St.Palais

Tables and benches in the open and among trees. Suitable for picnicking.Very pleasant. Recommended.
SOS — at the side.

Aire de St.Ciers

Partly forested, partly open space. Tables and benches , very pretty. Recommended.
SOS — at the entry.

80

12

143

13 51

St.Jean-d'Angely
Surgeres

130

+GPL

34

13

117

10

Gend 500 m   Saintes, Rochefort

107

Restaurant
on the other side
of the m-way.

11

96

Open; winter 7.00-22.15
summer 6.30-23.15
Tel. 4694-2530

11

Cognac, Pons

85

48

8

77

14

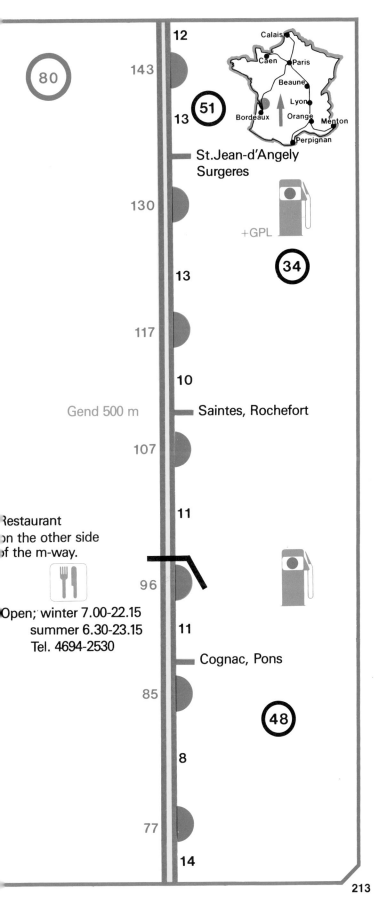

Aire de Coulombiers-Sud

Tables and benches. Open type of area, lit at night.
Swings, lot of grass. Recommended.
SOS — at the side of Area.

Aire de Rouillé-Pamproux

Tables and benches in the open and in shady spots.
Swings, lot of grass, good picnicking facilities.
SOS — at the side. Info-Route.

Aire de Ste. Eanne-Sud

Tables and benches. Lit at night. Swings, climbing things,
some shady spots. Recommended.
SOS — at the side.

Aire de Ste. Néomaye-Sud

Tables and benches. Spacious pleasant and
recommended.
SOS - at the side of area.

Aire des Les Ruralies

Tables and benches, shady spots. The other side of the
m-way's services accessible by a tunnel (cars go). Very
complex Area. Strongly recommended. SOS – at the side

Aire de Gript-Sud

Small, open type, tables and benches. Slides, swings,
climbing things. Nice.
SOS — at the exit.

Aire de Doeuil s/le Mignon

Tables and benches, climbing things. Shady spots.
SOS — at the exit

Poitiers -Sud

88

231

14

14

(Gendarmerie)

45

217

10

Lusignan

207

A10

36

14

193

12

St.Maixént

+GPL

e page
17

Tel. 4975-6676

181

Gend 2000 m

12

Niort, Nantes

169

14

51

155

12

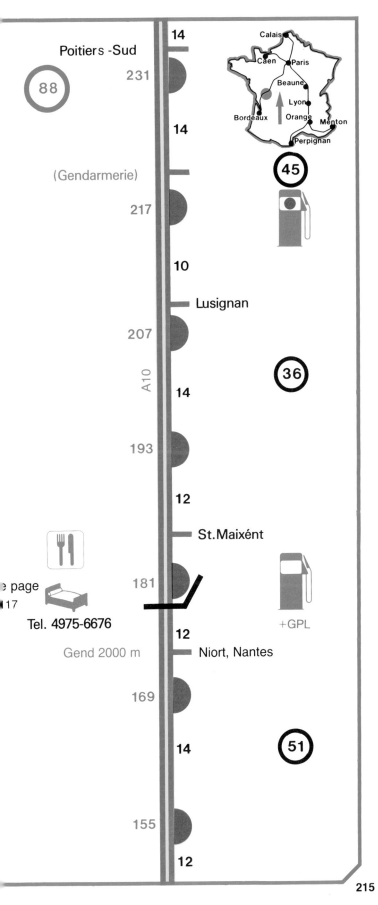

Aire de Barrière de péage

Few tables and benches
SOS — just past the Area.

Aire de Fontaine-Colette

Basically, just parking facilities.
SOS — at the side of Area.

Aire de Nouâtre

Few tables and benches among trees.
SOS — at the side.

Aire de Châtellerault Usseau

Extensive car parking facilities, bar, buffet, cafeteria, self-service.
SOS — at the side.

Aire des Chagnats

Quite a few benches among trees, very small and pleasant.
SOS — at the side of Area.

Aire de Poitiers Chince

Just parking facilities. Bar, buffet.
SOS – at the side towards the exit.
Well stocked shop including maps & guides

Aire des Quatre Vents

Few tables and benches. Rather nice.
SOS – just past the exit.

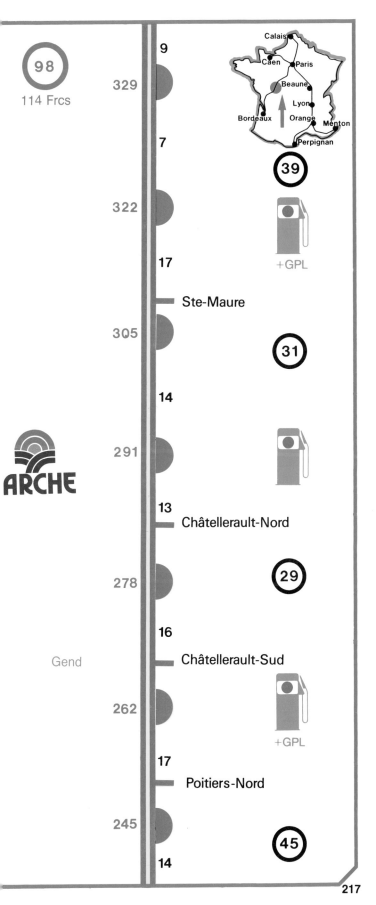

98
114 Frcs

ARCHE

Gend

9
329
7
322
17
Ste-Maure
305
14
291
13
Châtellerault-Nord
278
16
Châtellerault-Sud
262
17
Poitiers-Nord
245
14

Calais
Caen   Paris
Beaune
Lyon
Bordeaux   Orange
Menton
Perpignan

39

+GPL

31

29

+GPL

45

217

Aire de **Brusolle**

Tables and benches. Pretty.
SOS — at the side.

Aire de **Blois-Ménars**

Just parking spaces. Cafeteria with slides for children at
the side.
SOS – 200 m before entry.

Aire des **Bruères**

Open type of Area with tables and benches. Very small
and pleasant.
SOS – 200 m before entry.

Aire de la **Picardière**

A lot of tables and benches among trees, area located in
a little forest.
SOS – 500 m past the area.

Aire de **Barrière de péage**

Just parking facilities.
SOS — 400 m past the Area.

Aire de **Tours-Val-de-Loire**

Footbridge to the other side of the motorway's Rest Area.
Bar, buffet, boutique.
SOS — at the side by the entry. Info-Route.

Aire du **Moulin Rouge**

Forested, with tables and benches among trees. Lot of
grassy area, yet a good hiding place during hot weather
days. Interesting.
SOS — at the side of Area.

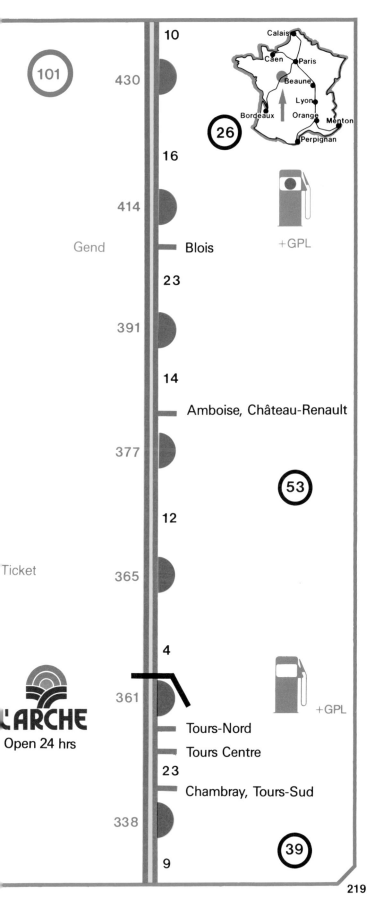

101

430

26

16

414

Gend

Blois

+GPL

23

391

14

Amboise, Château-Renault

377

53

12

Ticket

365

4

L'ARCHE
Open 24 hrs

361

+GPL

Tours-Nord

Tours Centre

23

Chambray, Tours-Sud

338

39

9

10

Calais
Caen · Paris
Beaune
Lyon
Bordeaux · Orange · Menton
Perpignan

219

Aire de Barrière de péage

Just parking spaces.
SOS – just by the line of péage.

Aire des Marnieres

Small with a few tables and benches.
SOS – 600 m past the area.

Aire du Val-Neuvy

Just parking facilities. Bar, buffet.

Aire de la Dauneuse

Dense forest with tables and benches amongst.
SOS — at the side of Area.

Aire d Orléans-Gidy

Cafeteria, grill, boutique. Just parking facilities.
SOS — at the side.

Aire de Chauvry

Tables and benches, some shady spots. Very small and nice.
SOS — at the entry.

Aire de Beaugency-Messas

Just parking facilities.
SOS — 300 m past the Area.

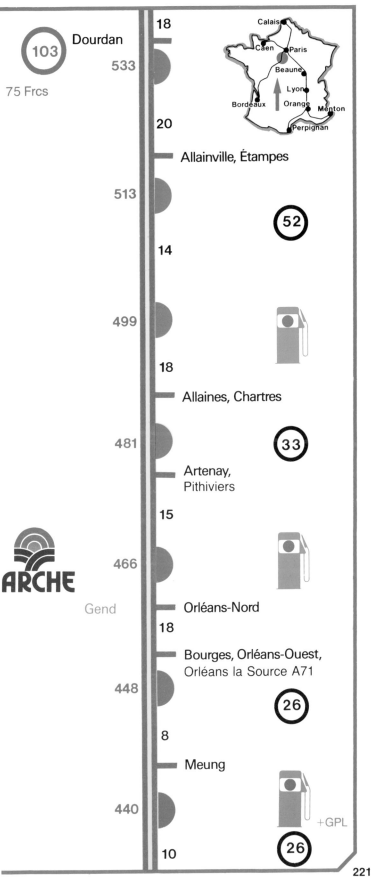

103 Dourdan
75 Frcs

18
533

20
Allainville, Étampes

513

14

499

18
Allaines, Chartres

52

481
Artenay,
Pithiviers

33

15

466

ARCHE

Gend
Orléans-Nord
18
Bourges, Orléans-Ouest,
Orléans la Source A71

448
26

8
Meung

440
+GPL

10
26

HOTEL MERCURE ＊＊＊

Autorute Lille - Dunkerque
Sortie Lomme - 59320 Englos
Tel.2092-3015, Telex:820 320 F

 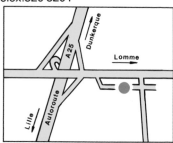

90 rooms with bathrooms or showers WC ● direct telephone line ●
colour TV ● radio ● mini-bar ● playing area for children ● nearby
tennis court ● terrace ● parking facilities.

Approaching the Boulevard Periphérique from the
direction of the Autoroute A6,(which is applicable to both;
coming from Bordeaux and from the Riviera) and
depending on your destination, you continue your journey
using the following information accordingly;-

At the first opportunity you select "Paris — Sud" and
follow "Paris" all the way.

Next, you have a choice; "Paris — Ouest" and "Paris —
Est". In case you missed it, there will be another choice
of the same, but this time the alternatives are more specific;
"Paris Ouest, Pte. Orléans" and "Paris — Est, Pte. d'Italie".
The same option will be offered to you once again soon
after that, before you enter the Boulevard round Paris.
The above information and the diagrammatically shown
Boulevard on the next page are complementary and
together will help you through; nicely.

And finally; for CAEN you follow the sign "ROUEN", and
for CALAIS you follow the sign "LILLE" while on the
Boulevard Periphérique.

Needless to say that for Caen you should always select
"Paris-Ouest" to begin with (much shorter).

Aire de Limours Bris s/s Forges

Just parking spaces. Buffet, bar.
SOS — at the side.

To continue your journey, turn over to page;-

224 — for Caen,
202 — for Calais

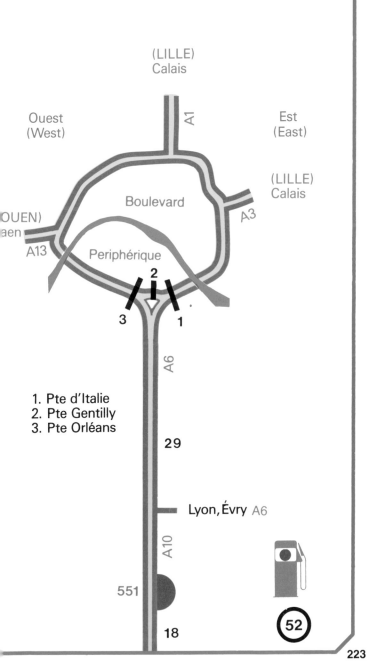

(LILLE)
Calais

Ouest
(West)

A1

Est
(East)

(LILLE)
Calais

Boulevard

A3

OUEN)
aen

A13

Periphérique

2

3   1

A6

1. Pte d'Italie
2. Pte Gentilly
3. Pte Orléans

29

Lyon, Évry   A6

A10

551

18

52

223

NO NAME

No facilities.

Few parking spaces.
SOS — close to the entry.

NO NAME

 — very basic

Very small and limited. Few parking spaces.
SOS — close to the exit.

Aire de **Morainvilliers**

Interconnected with the other side of the m-way service area
by a footbridge.
SOS — located close to the entry.

ALTEA VAL-DE-REUIL ★ ★ ★
Lieu — dit "Les Clouets" (Rouen)
Tel.3259-0909, Telex:180540

58 rooms with bathrooms ●
TV ● mini-bar ● restaurant ●
bar ● heated swimming pool ●
two tennis courts ● 4 conference
rooms ● golf and horse riding
near bay ● parking.

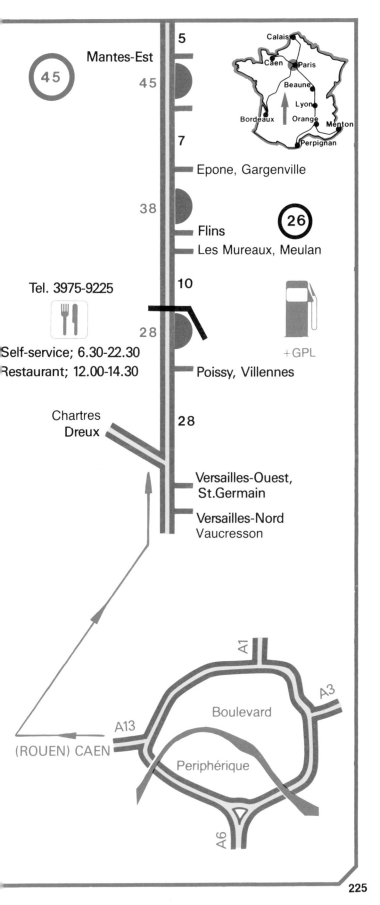

45

Mantes-Est

5

45

7

Epone, Gargenville

38

26

Flins
Les Mureaux, Meulan

10

Tel. 3975-9225

🍴

28

Self-service; 6.30-22.30
Restaurant; 12.00-14.30

+GPL

Poissy, Villennes

Chartres
Dreux

28

Versailles-Ouest,
St.Germain

Versailles-Nord
Vaucresson

A1

A3

Boulevard

A13

(ROUEN) CAEN

Periphérique

A6

Calais
Caen Paris
Beaune
Lyon
Bordeaux Orange
Menton
Perpignan

Aire de Vironvay

Interconnected with the other side of the Motorway's Services. Cafeteria, self-service.
SOS — close to the entry.

Aire de Barrière de péage

Just parking spaces. Simple.
Exit slip road and the entry to the rest area as one.

Aire de Beauchêne

Small, forested with few tables and benches.
SOS — by the entry.

Aire Nord de Douains

Few benches among trees. Very small, rather pleasant.
SOS — at the side of Area.

Aire Nord de la Villeneuve en Chevrie

Open space, grassy, some trees. Tables and benches.
Small, best so far.
SOS — at the side of Area.

Aire de Rosny/Seine

SOS — at the side of the area.
Well stocked boutique including maps & guides.

Aire de Barrière de péage

Just parking facilities.

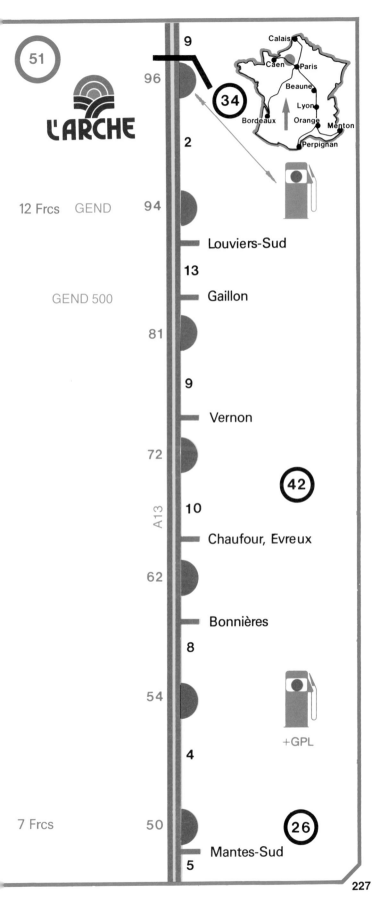

51

L'ARCHE

34

9

96

2

12 Frcs   GEND

94

Louviers-Sud

13

GEND 500

Gaillon

81

9

Vernon

72

42

A13

10

Chaufour, Evreux

62

Bonnières

8

54

+GPL

4

7 Frcs   50

26

Mantes-Sud

5

Calais
Caen   Paris
Beaune
Lyon
Bordeaux   Orange
Menton
Perpignan

Aire d' Annebault

Open type space, grassy, some trees. Tables and benches.
Small, isolated from the Motorway by a wall of trees. Very
pleasant.
SOS — 100 m from the entry.

Aire Nord de Beuzeville

Exstensive parking facilities, grassy. Some trees, tables and
benches, spacious and attractive.
SOS — at the side.

Aire de Barrière de péage

Just parking spaces.

Aire de Josapha

Open space type of area. Few tables and benches. Very
pleasant.
SOS — 200 m from the entry.

Aire de Bosgouet

Cafeteria, snack bar. Interconnected with the other side
Rest Area.
SOS — located close to the entry of the Rest Area.

Aire Nord de Robert-le-Diable

Open space type of area, very small.
SOS — located by the exit.

Aire de Bord

Small, grassy, tables and benches. Nice.
SOS — at the side of Area.

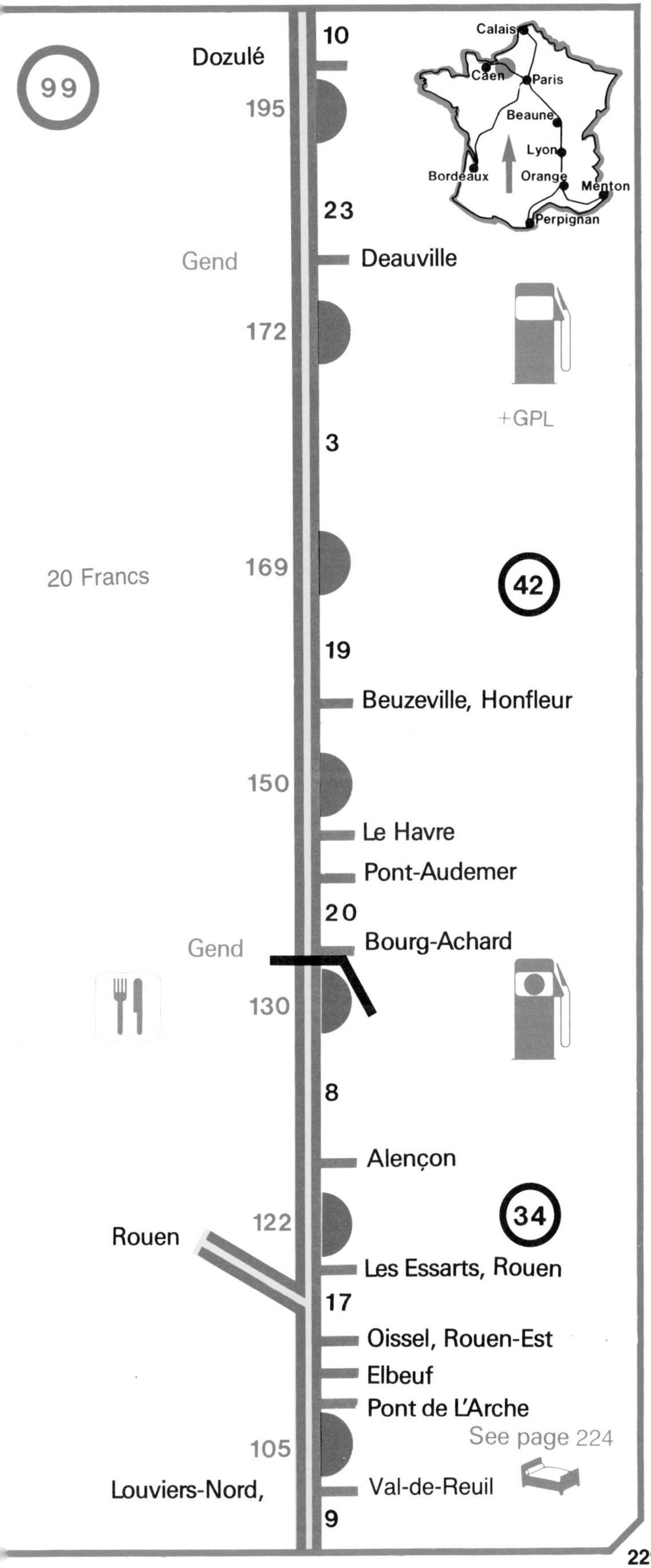

99
10
Dozulé
195
Calais
Caen
Paris
Beaune
Lyon
Bordeaux
Orange
Menton
Perpignan
23
Gend
Deauville
172
+GPL
3
169
20 Francs
42
19
Beuzeville, Honfleur
150
Le Havre
Pont-Audemer
20
Gend
Bourg-Achard
130
8
Alençon
122
34
Rouen
Les Essarts, Rouen
17
Oissel, Rouen-Est
Elbeuf
Pont de L'Arche
See page 224
105
Louviers-Nord,
Val-de-Reuil
9

HOTEL MERCURE ***

Port de Plaisance, Centre Ville - Place Courtonne,
14000 – Caen
Tel.3193-0762, Telex:171890, Fax.3147-4388.

 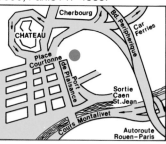

101 rooms with bathrooms ● TV with video circuit, canal + ● radio ●
mini-bar ● restaurant ● bar ● private parking facilities.

HOTEL NOVOTEL BAYEUX ***

Rond Point de Vaucelles,
14400 – Bayeux
Tel.3192-1611, Telex:170176

 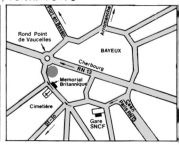

78 rooms with bathrooms ● radio ● TV with canal + ● mini-bar ● grill
● swimming pool ● garden ● golf course - 8 km ● parking facilities.

Aire Nord de Giberville

Few tables and benches. Spacious.
SOS — at the side.

Aire de Barrière de péage

Just sort of a bay, no parking facilities.

HOTEL IBIS **
Parc des Expositions,
76800 – Rouen-Sud
Tel.3566-0363, Telex:771014

 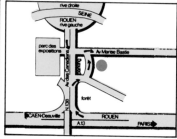

108 rooms with bathrooms ● radio ● TV ● restaurant ● grill ● parking facilities.

According to the French Police records, about 50% of all accidents involving British cars, takes place within 80 km of the Channel. Do not rush. take care.

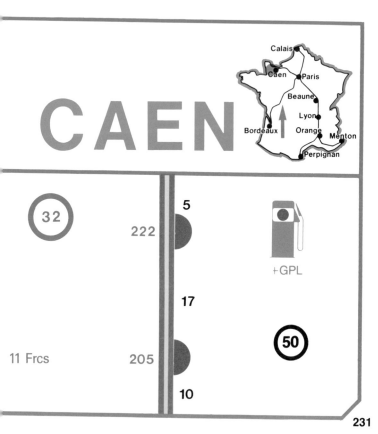

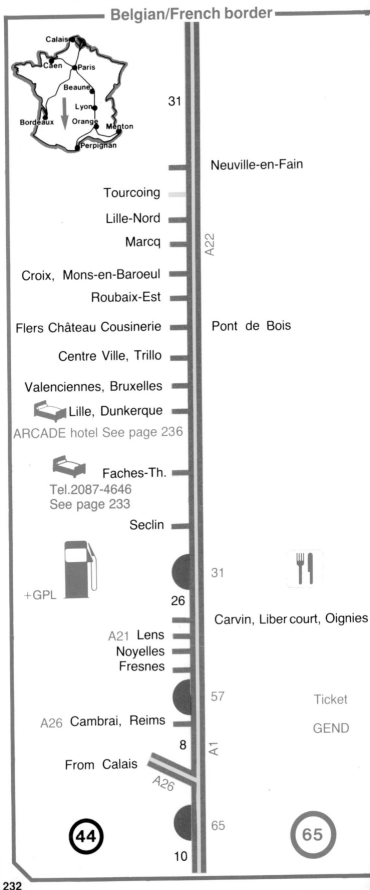

Belgian/French border

Calais
Caen — Paris
Beaune
Lyon
Bordeaux — Orange — Menton
Perpignan

31

Neuville-en-Fain

Tourcoing

Lille-Nord

Marcq

A22

Croix, Mons-en-Baroeul

Roubaix-Est

Flers Château Cousinerie — Pont de Bois

Centre Ville, Trillo

Valenciennes, Bruxelles

Lille, Dunkerque

ARCADE hotel See page 236

Faches-Th.

Tel.2087-4646
See page 233

Seclin

+GPL

31

26

Carvin, Liber court, Oignies

A21 Lens
Noyelles
Fresnes

57

Ticket

A26 Cambrai, Reims

GEND

8

A1

From Calais

A26

44

65

65

10

HOTEL MERCURE * * *

110 rue Jean Jaures
59810 Lesquin
Tel.2087-4646, Telex:132051, Fax:2087-4647

 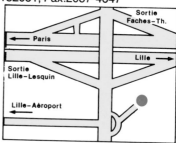

213 rooms with fully equipped bathrooms ● direct telephone line ●
colour TV ● mini-bar ● in-door heated swimming pool ● sauna ● bar
● grill ● restaurant ● conference rooms ● parking facilities.

Aire de **Phalempin-Ouest**

Generally parking facilities. The main items of the boutique; maps & guides,toiletries,cassettes,CB radios,foods &
drinks,newspapers & magazines.

Aire de **Barrière de péage**

Just parking facilities.

Aire de **Wancourt-Ouest**

This rest area's name is shown here for your reference
only.
To continue for Paris turn to page 88.

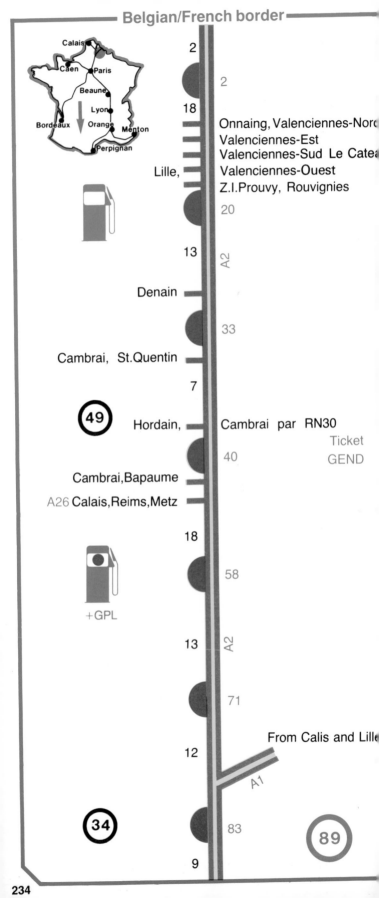

2

2

18

Onnaing, Valenciennes-Nord
Valenciennes-Est
Valenciennes-Sud Le Catea
Lille,   Valenciennes-Ouest
Z.I.Prouvy, Rouvignies

20

13   A2

Denain

33

Cambrai, St.Quentin

7

49

Hordain,   Cambrai par RN30

Ticket
GEND

40

Cambrai,Bapaume

A26 Calais,Reims,Metz

18

58

+GPL

13   A2

71

From Calis and Lille

12

A1

34

83

89

9

234

Aire des Enclosis

Open type two lane rest area, partly forested. There are tables and benches. Very nice.
SOS – at the side of area.

Aire de la Sentinelle

Spacious. The shop is well stocked with; maps & guides, hygiene items, perfumes and obviously with drinks foods etc.. Bar, buffet.
SOS – at the side of area.

Aire d' Hordain

One lane parking, few benches, lit, slightly forested.
SOS – at side of area.

Aire de Barrière de péage

Upper part of the rest area with tables and benches. Very pleasant.

Aire de Graincourt

There is a well stocked shop with items like; maps & guide books, foods, toys, gifts etc. Hot drinks available from automatic machines. There are tables are benches.
SOS – at the side of the area.

Aire de Barastre

Two lane parking facilities, not lit. Tables and benches. Small and pleasant.
SOS – at the side of area.

Aire de Maurepas

This rest area's name is shown here for your reference only.
To continue for Paris turn over to page 88.

HOTEL ARCADE LILLE **

172 Rue de Paris   59800 – Lille   Tel.2030-0054, Telex: 136 54.

140 rooms, all with shower and WC • telephone • colour TV on request • automatic morning call • restaurant • bar • parking fcilities • easy access to the motorway network.

Aire de **Phalempin-Est**

Just parking facilities.
SOS – located 200 m past the rest area.

Aire de **Barrière de péage**

Just parking facilities. Spacious.

Aire de **Wancourt-Est**

This rest area's name is shown here for your reference only.

Continued from Paris, page 206.

68

232

32

Neuville-en-Fain

Tourcoing-Nord

Roncq

Tourcoing-Ouest

Marcq-en-Boeuil

Croix, Mons, Wasquehal

Roubaix

Flers Château Cousinerie

Pony de Bois

Triolo

Cysoning

A22

A27(A23), Tournai, Liége, Bruxelles, Valenciennes

To continue page 240

Lille- Lesquin

Seclin

199

+GPL

Libercourt, Oignies Carvin

Henin-Bt., Lens, A21

A1

26

Noyelles-Godault

Fresnes, Douai

Francs
ND

173

8

Calais, Reims, Cambrai

A26

L'Arageois

42

165

24/24

Arras-Est

A1

8

237

Aire de Emblise

Just parking facilities. Pleasant.

Aire de la Sentinelle

Basically parking facilities. Hot drinks available from automatic machines.
Exit slip road and the entry road to the rest area as one.
SOS -- at the side of area.

Aire de Lieu St-Amand

One lane parking, few benches.
SOS – at the side of area.

Aire de Barrière de Péage

Small with limited parking facilities.

Aire d' Havrincourt

Small, tables and benches, cafeteria, grill.
Well stocked boutique. Recommended.

Aire de Rocquigny

Tables and benches, some trees, small.
SOS – at the side of the area.

Aire de Feuilléres

This rest area's name is shown here for your reference only.
Continued from Paris, page 206.